Progressive Nationalism

Citizenship and the Left

David Goodhart

DEMOS

DEM©S

About Demos

Who we are

Demos is the think tank for everyday democracy. We believe everyone should be able to make personal choices in their daily lives that contribute to the common good. Our aim is to put this democratic idea into practice by working with organisations in ways that make them more effective and legitimate.

What we work on

We focus on six areas: public services; science and technology; cities and public space; people and communities; arts and culture; and global security.

Who we work with

Our partners include policy-makers, companies, public service providers and social entrepreneurs. Demos is not linked to any party but we work with politicians across political divides. Our international network – which extends across Eastern Europe, Scandinavia, Australia, Brazil, India and China – provides a global perspective and enables us to work across borders.

How we work

Demos knows the importance of learning from experience. We test and improve our ideas in practice by working with people who can make change happen. Our collaborative approach means that our partners share in the creation and ownership of new ideas.

What we offer

We analyse social and political change, which we connect to innovation and learning in organisations. We help our partners show thought leadership and respond to emerging policy challenges.

How we communicate

As an independent voice, we can create debates that lead to real change. We use the media, public events, workshops and publications to communicate our ideas. All our books can be downloaded free from the Demos website.

www.demos.co.uk

First published in 2006
© Demos
Some rights reserved – see copyright licence for details

ISBN 1 84180 159 3
Copy edited by Julie Pickard, London
Typeset and printed by Upstream, London

For further information and
subscription details please contact:

Demos
Magdalen House
136 Tooley Street
London SE1 2TU

telephone: 0845 458 5949
email: hello@demos.co.uk
web: www.demos.co.uk

Contents

Acknowledgements

This pamphlet has been brewing for almost 18 months and is, in part, meant as the political coda to the issues raised in my *Prospect* essay 'Too diverse?' (subsequently reprinted in the *Guardian*) of February 2004. Thanks are due to many people – some of whom are listed below – who either read and commented on the pamphlet itself or said useful things on the broad subject in private conversation or seminar rooms:

Vidhya Alakeson, Douglas Alexander, Rushanara Ali, Christopher Caldwell, Matt Cavanagh, Linda Colley, Barry Cox, Jon Cruddas, Geoff Dench, John Denham, Patrick Diamond, Bobby Duffy, Catherine Fieschi, Charles Grant, Krishna Guha, Robert Hazell, Lucy Heller, David Herman, Will Hutton, Robert Jackson, Sunder Katwala, Eric Kaufmann, Lucy Kellaway, David Lammy, Anatol Lieven, Michael Lind, Alex Linklater, John Lloyd, Michael Maclay, Denis MacShane, Kenan Malik, Ehsan Masood, Tariq Modood, Anshuman Mondal, David Miller, Geoff Mulgan, Toby Mundy, Kamran Nazeer, Paul Ormerod, Bhikhu Parekh, Nick Pearce, Trevor Phillips, Michael Prowse, Robert Putnam, Chakravarthi Ram-Prasad, Ben Rogers, Ann Rossiter, Bob Rowthorn, Shamit Saggar, John Salt, Roger Scruton, Paul Skidmore, Adrian Smith, Danny Sriskandarajah, Peter Taylor-Gooby, David Walker, David Willetts and Mari Williams.

Thanks, in particular, to the team at Demos – Tom Bentley, Catherine Fieschi, Sam Hinton-Smith and Julia Huber – for publishing the pamphlet so professionally.

David Goodhart
May 2006

Summary

Politicians of the centre-left in Britain, and elsewhere in Europe, are trying to raise the visibility of national citizenship in response to growing anxieties about identity and migration in our more fluid societies – but they often do so defensively and uncertainly. Britain does need a clearer idea of citizenship and a robust protection of the privileges and entitlements associated with it. Indeed, an inclusive, progressive, civic British nationalism – comfortable with Britain's multiethnic and multiracial character and its place in the European Union (EU) – is the best hope for preserving the social democratic virtues embodied in a generous welfare state and a thriving public domain. This pamphlet seeks to establish a more coherent and confident basis for centre-left thinking on the nation state and citizenship. It then sketches a framework for conceiving national citizenship in Britain today and how it might be revived, with a central role for the welfare state. It ends with some general policy suggestions.

1. The rise of security and identity issues

In the past few years the cluster of issues that are grouped together under the heading 'security and identity' have started to matter more to voters and politicians across Europe. The category includes (with different emphasis in different places) terrorism; asylum and immigration; the integration of minorities, especially significant Muslim minorities; the power of the EU, national sovereignty and regionalism; violent crime (or the fear of it); rising incivility; and the changing character of local communities.

The security and identity issues in Europe are not an invention of the media; they have emerged in response to real events such as economic globalisation (and cultural Americanisation), the recent terrorist attacks in Europe, the sharp rise in asylum-led immigration starting in the early 1990s, the continuing arguments about the speed and desirability of European integration, devolution within many of the historic nation states of Europe, and most recently the place of Islam in Europe. The higher profile of these 'who are we?' and 'how can we live together?' issues also reflects the declining force of class-based distributional issues and the state versus market cold-war-related conflict that dominated European politics in the second half of the twentieth century. Indeed, partly thanks to the new salience of security and identity issues and the populist parties that have emerged to exploit them the main political party of the left no longer commands a majority of the working-class vote in Belgium, France, Italy or the Netherlands. Fears connected with external competition and migration were also central to the 'no' votes in the EU constitution referendums in France and the Netherlands. A 'new politics' that cuts across established left–right boundaries has emerged.

In Britain there has been no equivalent of Jean Marie Le Pen or Pim Fortuyn but here too security and identity issues emerged from a position of very low visibility ten years ago to fill two of the top three places on voters' lists of the 'most important issues' in 2005 (according to MORI the most important issue was defence and terrorism, the second most important was the National Health Service (NHS) and the third most important was race and immigration). The British National Party (BNP) won more than 800,000 votes in the last European elections, and it is common to hear Labour MPs worrying about the attitudes of their 'left behind' white working-class constituents – and all this at a time of unusually benign economic conditions. (This pamphlet went to press before the 4 May local elections in which the BNP was expected to perform strongly.) Less dramatic than the rise of the BNP is the prospect of a slow but growing divergence between London (and thus the national media) and a few other big cities, which are significantly and, in the main, comfortably multiethnic, and whole regions of the country (such as the north east and the south west) plus small town and rural Britain, which remain ethnically homogeneous and far more culturally conservative. Furthermore, despite the relatively calm response to the London bombs it is hard to believe that 7/7 will not keep security and identity themes at the forefront of political debate for years to come. The issue of Islamic extremism does unavoidably spill over into the wider debate about immigration and asylum – although, more positively, it has also given a fresh impetus to careful thinking about how to foster a renewed sense of Britishness. The latter has been in decline in recent decades as a result of Scottish and Welsh devolution but also thanks to the fading of those forces – such as the empire and Protestantism – that helped to create and define the first 250 years of Britishness.

Renewing the story of Britishness is an urgent political task for the centre-left. Most people assume, not unreasonably, that the rise of security and identity issues will benefit the political right (both moderate and extreme right) with its claim to speak with the nation's ancestral voices. But with the application of some hard-headed liberalism this advantage can be neutralised and, through a renewed commitment to the idea of a national *community*, these issues can even be turned to the advantage of the centre-left. When people feel secure about themselves and their societies they are likely to feel more generous towards outsiders, both at home and abroad. There is nothing politically dishonourable about responding to widely held anxieties. Indeed, measures that reassure people, especially the least well off and most vulnerable, that their interests and traditions are not being lost sight of in a more mobile and diverse world are more progressive in their effect than vague expressions of internationalism and pleas for tolerance.

As Wouter Bos, the Dutch Labour leader, has written in *Prospect*:

We could leave the dilemmas [of diversity] unacknowledged. Those of us on the centre-left in the Netherlands know where that got us: look at the historic defeat of the left in the 2002 elections, look at the hardening of the debate on migration that followed, look at how little is left of the tolerance and liberty that Dutch society was once famous for. Leaving this debate to the right may feel comfortable because we will not have to disappoint anybody and it will enable us to continue promising everything to everybody. But . . . this will not help those who count on us. It won't help the newcomers to our society who are promised a future that we cannot provide. And it won't help the long-established citizens . . . who will suffer from the slow erosion of collective arrangements. This debate cannot be ignored by the progressive side of politics. It is our debate too.[1]

2. Reclaiming the national story

The centre-left has in the past been more politically vulnerable over security and identity issues than it needs to be. This is partly because progressive thought has been influenced by a set of myths or half-truths. There are three in particular.

First is the fallacy that human beings are egalitarian individualists with a tendency to treat all other humans with equal regard. The idea that all human life should be sacred and that all humans should be treated with respect does not mean that we have equal feelings or commitments to all humanity. In economics and sociology the left embraces the idea of group interests and affinities. But when it comes to culture or national sentiment the left switches to a rhetoric of individualism, implicitly seeing society – or at least the dominant culture – as no more than a collection of individuals with no special ties towards each other. This 'blank sheet' individualism often employs the language of internationalism and universalism, increasingly the preferred discourse of elites (of both left and right) in contrast to the economic and cultural communitarianism of most ordinary people.

Second is the fallacy that nationalism and national feeling is only and necessarily a belligerent and xenophobic force. National feeling has always been janus-like. Alongside the hatred it has generated it is also responsible for many of the most positive aspects of modern societies – the idea of equal citizenship, the readiness to share with and make sacrifices for stranger-citizens, the strong feelings of belonging and membership beyond one's own kin group that it generates. Feelings of *national* solidarity can be regarded as a more intense subset of the more general feeling of *human* solidarity – both are about identifying with and empathising with strangers. There is no reason why the two sentiments should necessarily be seen as antagonistic or mutually exclusive, even if in the past 500 years they have often been pitted against each other.[2]

BILL PROUD

'How can immigrants integrate
into society if there's no such thing as society?'

It was sentiments of national solidarity as much as class solidarity, a feeling that 'we are all in this together', that helped to build and sustain the welfare state. It is the core belief of the left, against the individualism of free-market liberals, that there is such a thing as society – but in the modern world <u>that always, everywhere, means a specific national society.</u> The left is often in the odd position of liking the idea of society in the abstract but disliking the reality of any specific national society with its exclusive national interests and 'irrational' national egoism. George Monbiot writing in the *Guardian* is typical: 'Patriotism . . . tells us we should favour the interests of 100 British people over 101 Congolese. How do you reconcile this choice with liberalism? How for that matter do you distinguish it from racism?'[3] Monbiot's caricature of patriotism belongs to the imperial age when might was right, when there were zero-sum trade-offs between colonised and coloniser and western nations considered themselves morally and racially superior. In its place he seems to want a world in which no one comes from anywhere – in which we have no greater commitment to our neighbours and fellow citizens than someone who lives the other side of the world. This is not only an unrealistic picture, it is also an unattractive one. Fortunately zero-sum colonial brutality and country-blind cosmopolitanism are not the only two options.

[margin handwritten note:] No,

The third fallacy, following on from the second, is the belief that western countries, especially those like Britain with a colonial past, are responsible for most of the ills of developing countries and can best make amends by placing as few obstacles as possible in the way of people from those countries coming to live in the west. The legacy of colonialism is complex and varied. Many terrible things were done by western colonisers over 500 years, many benign things too. But prior to the very recent past almost all powerful civilisations – including Islamic ones – have embraced slavery and conquest; we should be careful not to judge the past by the standards of the present. Historical guilt aside, it is, in any case, hardly an advantage for contemporary developing countries to lose their best educated and most energetic people to the west.

Sensible policy cannot be made on the basis of the three fallacies above. Moreover, the left needs to acknowledge in a more clear-eyed way two 'progressive dilemmas' thrown up by modern politics. In an essay I wrote in *Prospect* I described the first dilemma as the tension between solidarity and diversity.[4] The argument is simply that the more different we become from one another – the more diverse our ways of life and our religious and ethnic backgrounds – and the less we share a moral consensus or a sense of fellow feeling, the less happy we will be in the long run to support a generous welfare state. One should not exaggerate the degree of homogeneity or moral consensus that existed in, say, 1950s Britain, nor the *inevitability* of a growth in diversity translating into an unwillingness to share. But coming on top of all the other strains on the welfare state, from rising individual affluence to an ageing society, it would be foolish for the centre-left not to keep a close watch on the interaction between diversity and welfare over the coming decades.

The second progressive dilemma or tension arises in relation to the nation state itself. The left has historically struggled for a 'universal' notion of equal national citizenship that is blind to wealth, status, gender and, more recently, race and ethnicity, and one that promotes a high degree of sharing and engagement with our fellow citizens. Yet this idea of citizenship is not universal at all; it stops at our borders. Nations have boundaries. Citizenship must include *and* exclude. Notwithstanding the much greater international interconnectedness of modern life, we continue to favour our fellow national citizens over those of other countries – consider the fact that we spend 25 times more each year on the NHS than on development aid. This does not mean, contrary to Monbiot, that we regard British people as morally superior to Congolese people. Nor does it mean that we have no obligations towards humanity as a whole, and especially towards the citizens of former colonial countries that we exploited in the past.

But those obligations do not require us to sacrifice the traditions and coherence of our own societies or to offer British citizenship to anyone who wants it – we should express our solidarity with those in poor countries mainly through aid, fair trade rules and a just asylum system. These things represent only a fraction of the mutuality expressed in the political, legal, economic and welfare rights and duties which bind us to our fellow national citizens – but they are not insignificant. Moreover, it is quite possible to imagine a world of cooperating nation states successfully addressing, over time, today's global imbalances in wealth and power. In fact, it is easier to imagine cooperating nation states achieving this goal in roughly their current form than as postnational entities that have abolished themselves in favour of a mirage of global citizenship or government.

A government's first priority must be to its own citizens – all of them. This may seem obvious enough but it often collides with the assumptions of the internationalist left (and the business elite) as well as the xenophobic right (who refuse to recognise the non-indigenous as full citizens). The uncomfortable truth to many progressives – and something which the explicit universalism of the Human Rights Act sometimes blurs – is that the modern nation state is based not on a universalist liberalism but on a contractual idea of club membership. This is neither arbitrary nor necessarily based on prejudice. If we offered the national rights we enjoy to the rest of humanity – through, for example, having no immigration controls at all – they would quickly become worthless, especially those welfare rights with a financial cost attached that progressives value so highly. And it also follows from a progressive notion of citizenship that we should be far from indifferent about who becomes a fellow citizen. Yet a studied indifference about who is migrating to Britain has in the past been a distinguishing characteristic of progressive belief. (A typical example can be found in the recent report on migration by the RSA, which declared that any attempt to favour higher-skilled immigrants over lower-skilled ones was 'reminiscent of South Africa's apartheid regime'.[5])

Security and identity issues of course throw up many complex and difficult questions about citizenship and membership. But two basic points for the centre-left are surely clear.

First, security and identity issues should mainly be seen as questions about *community*. By placing these issues so high on their list of priorities many voters are expressing a fear of rapid change but they are also sending a broader signal about how important they continue to regard the idea of society and citizenship, and are implicitly rejecting the idea of society as nothing more than a collection of individuals.

Second, greater mobility and value diversity mean that the everyday reciprocities and conventions that once underpinned membership of the local or national community are no longer so self-evident. We no longer support people in need because they are 'one of us' and our fathers/grandfathers fought together in the same wars, but rather because they are encompassed by a more formal citizenship–welfare contract. That means the nature of the British citizenship–welfare contract and the behaviour of political actors needs to be spelt out more explicitly. One recent example of this was the establishment in 1994 of the Nolan committee into standards in public life – people could no longer be assumed to understand automatically what those standards were. Many of the social, political and welfare rights of British citizenship are already 'contractual' in the sense of being conditional on appropriate behaviour – even if that behaviour is as basic as agreeing to abide by the law or the unemployed being ready to seek work in return for welfare support. This 'rights and responsibilities' or 'something for something' approach to domestic issues has been a central plank of New Labour's mainstream appeal. It now needs to be extended more overtly from established citizens to new citizens, too, if governments are to win political legitimacy for significant levels of immigration. And a clearer 'offer' of British citizenship needs to be made both to aid integration and to reassure existing citizens of the value of their own membership.

These last two points stake out a territory that the centre-left can confidently make its own, as it seeks to channel feelings of national belonging in a benign direction and away from the xenophobia and racism that is the expression of communal feelings turned sour. Over the past few decades there has been a dramatic decline in big, defining frameworks in peoples' lives, whether national or religious. A sense of national belonging has often been replaced by the idea of individual self-actualisation or by narrower group identities. And the idea of the national political community extending rights and obligations over time (and as a result of many struggles) to all citizens has been replaced by the thin and ahistorical notion of human rights. The good society needs deeper commitments than that.

Yet many people on the left would regard the idea of a 'progressive nationalism' as an oxymoron (except when applied to the anti-colonial struggles of small or developing countries). Nationalism was, of course, a highly destructive force in European society in the first half of the twentieth century. But war within Europe, at least between the big powers, is unthinkable in 2006. Feelings of national solidarity can coexist comfortably with many other ethnic, class or regional identities. It is true that in the past such national feeling was intensified through confrontation with other nations but it does not require such confrontation. The centre-left cannot afford to be squeamish about national feeling; the alternative to a mild, progressive nationalism is not internationalism, which will always be a minority creed, but either chauvinistic nationalism or the absence of any broader solidarities at all.

It is a tiresome truism to say that people have multiple identities and allegiances; they always have done. However multiple and hybrid their identities people still need to connect to the wider social and political entities of which they are a part. Indeed, as affluence and individualism weakens the other collective identities of class, ethnicity and religion (at least for the British majority), feelings of national identity may be the last resting place for the collective commitments that the left holds dear. This does not mean ignoring or downplaying distributional conflicts between groups within the national society, especially when inequality has been growing as sharply as it has been in recent decades. Nor does it require an uncritical attitude to the nation or its history and symbols. The left has often, with justice, mocked the excesses of national vanity and antipathy to foreigners, and should continue to do so. Indeed, New Labour has been too uncritical of Britain's imperial past with both Tony Blair and Gordon Brown praising the British empire without qualification. But equally the left's uneasiness with British national feeling is itself, in part, an anachronistic hangover from the days of the empire and militarist jingoism. Those days are gone; national feeling can now be put to better use.

3. A new Britishness 'contract'

Reviving the idea of Britishness is easier said than done. Today, it is an idea in retreat. 'Britishness', as Anthony Heath has argued, 'may be particularly vulnerable to the processes of modernisation.'[6] This is because many of the things it was built on – empire, Protestantism, the labour and trades union movement, two world wars – are either fading from memory or are less significant than they used to be. Moreover, some of the things that distinguished Britain from much of continental Europe from the seventeenth to the twentieth century – liberty under the law and parliamentary democracy – are no longer uniquely British. Partly for these reasons, Britishness in recent years has seemed a less attractive concept to many Scottish and Welsh citizens, and younger people throughout Britain have less pride in its achievements as they fade from memory.

And, of course, unlike most 'classical' nationalisms where an ethnic nation coheres politically to form a state, Britain is (technically) not a nation at all but a state formed out of an amalgam of four nations. The English, partly because of their overwhelming dominance, have tended to confuse their own historic English nation with the British state – to the irritation of the Scots, Welsh and Northern Irish. But following the last wave of devolution the English have become more aware of the England–Britain distinction which has itself caused a limited revival of interest in Englishness.[7]

If British national citizenship is to be made more attractive again to members of its four ethnic nations, plus the large settled immigrant communities from south Asia, Africa and the West Indies, it will be partly because of the way it is modernised but also because it continues to answer a need for public identities and meanings. There is clearly a greater need for that in England than in Scotland, Wales or Northern Ireland, because of the relative absence of an institutionalised Englishness. But now that devolution has been negotiated successfully in Scotland and Wales, the recent decline in the preference for a British identity can perhaps be halted there, too. The Scots, Welsh and Northern Irish increase their influence and presence in the world through being part of Britain, just as Britain increases its clout through being part of the EU. There is also no inherent reason why there should be a zero-sum trade-off between increased attachment to, say, England or Scotland on the one hand and Britain on the other – even if the attachments have a somewhat different quality.

The need for a more visible, meaningful national story – especially for the English – also follows from the erosion of a more local, neighbourly belonging. Many people in Britain, especially those living in run-down areas, with little money and few opportunities, look back nostalgically on a time of more tightly knit and supportive communities. Since industrialisation and the growth of big cities this golden age has seldom actually existed. But various trends over the past 50 years have contributed to the retreat of strong micro-communities capable of generating feelings of stability and belonging. These include social and geographical mobility;[8] the erosion of collectivism and the working-class communities based around heavy industry; the decline of extended families; the sharp increase in income inequality and the apparent breakdown in the upward social escalator for lower income groups in some parts of the country; the effects of rapid immigration in some towns and cities; the rise of lifestyle and value diversity; and the decline of organised public belief. Much of this 'dehomogenisation' represents an increase in human freedom, but some of it has also come at the cost of eroding a sense of belonging both to small, local communities and to a broader national community. There is strong evidence to suggest that crime is lower and even health outcomes are better where people do have strong local attachments.[9] About 70 per cent of people say that they still feel a very or fairly strong sense of neighbourhood belonging but that number appears to be in long-term decline.[10]

Moreover, although many of the forces of modern life have been successfully designed to give citizens greater control of their destinies and their environments, the means by which that control is achieved, such as the increasingly globalised market economy or international institutions like the EU or World Trade Organization, leaves people with the feeling that their destinies are subject to forces outside their local or even national political communities. As a consequence of rising affluence and modern technology, most of us can control our *individual* destinies to a far greater extent than our parents or grandparents could but it may be that the price of such control is losing a clear sense of our *collective* destinies.

It is true that the ubiquity of the mass media and the sameness of many aspects of modern urban life act as countervailing forces to atomisation. We are less likely to know our neighbour but we are more likely to have something in common with any given stranger, because of the similarity of work and consumption patterns (in particular media consumption) across Britain. Nonetheless, the priority now given by voters to security and identity issues is an indicator that in the contest between fragmentation and homogenisation, many people think that fragmentation is winning and regret it. This fragmentation that is an inevitable consequence of modern life makes even more important an overt political rhetoric of British national identity and solidarity – it provides a kind of over-arching 'roof' under which the other more particular identities of class, region, religion and ethnicity can shelter.

Such a rhetoric should also help to ease the process of integration for new citizens. The recent debate about minority integration, initiated by Trevor Phillips, head of the Commission for Racial Equality, has perhaps been unduly gloomy because it is based on an unrealistic assumption about human affinities and the speed at which integration is likely to happen. Nevertheless, some of Phillips's anxiety about long-term trends is justified, at least for some minorities. When people of very different backgrounds come to live together one would expect some initial distrust, suspicion and even hostility. One would also expect time and shared experiences to iron out much of that friction (consider the large Irish integration into Britain over the past 150 years). But strong communities require continuity in space and time. I know that I can trust my neighbour regardless of markers of difference (such as accent or skin colour) because we have lived next door to each other for many years; he has sometimes helped me out and I have done the same for him and as a result we have a bank of positive shared experiences to draw on. But the modern world is very bad at creating this kind of trust-generating continuity and nation-building shared experience, either locally or nationally.

Many of the trends of the past 50 years (see above) have increased social distance and eroded moral consensus. And, as minority numbers rise and bring a critical mass of a particular minority in one area, it becomes easier *not* to integrate into mainstream society – especially for those minorities who bring sharply different worldviews. When a few hundreds of thousands of citizens opt to live in ethnic or religious enclaves it may not matter too much; when several million do there is a problem for social cohesion. Numbers do matter.

A progressive civic nationalism or integrationism for our more mobile and diverse age will look very different from the kind of nationalism that most British citizens would have instinctively signed up to in 1950. The English, Welsh and Scots were more socially hierarchical and ethnically homogeneous in 1950 than they are today; British political institutions were far less entwined in international institutions such as the EU; and in 1950 feelings of national solidarity were at a peak after 200 years of industrialisation, urbanisation, the creation of Britain itself and its empire, the emergence of democracy and mass literacy, and then the two world wars.

Some people argue that this feeling of national solidarity was a kind of historic blip – it had never existed before on such a large scale and it will never exist again as we evolve in a more individualistic and transnational direction, creating smaller communities of choice in contrast to the larger communities of fate. While it is surely true that it is neither possible nor desirable to re-create the often chauvinistic feelings of national membership that existed in the nineteenth century and the first half of the twentieth century, some general feeling of membership is still required to realise many of the goals of social democracy even in our more fluid and diverse societies.

It is important when thinking of a renewed British national citizenship to work primarily from the inside out, rather than placing too much of the weight on the manner in which we define *new* citizens – important though that is. For the roof of national identity and citizenship is not there only to act as a link between the majority and ethnic minorities. It is the glue that connects a working-class person and a middle-class person, someone from Yorkshire and a Londoner, a Scot and a Cornishman, and across the minority divide, say, a British Pakistani with a British Arab.

But what should this more open, renewed form of British membership look like? What should the state-citizen 'deal' look like in the early twenty-first century? The most important thing that Britain can offer to all its citizens is simply to be itself: to be rich, democratic, free and peaceful. The country must of course live up to its own laws and norms in terms of equality before the law and non-discrimination so that all citizens can take advantage of the economic opportunities and political freedoms on offer; it should also provide some special help to new citizens, or would-be citizens, to help them integrate (paying for language lessons for example or the mentoring of individuals by local volunteers) and make room for different cultural practices as far as possible in everyday life (providing prayer rooms for pious Muslims for example).

What should citizens, both old and new, agree to in return? To accept the rule of law and the legitimate authority of the state and its institutions (even while disagreeing passionately with all or part of what any particular government does); to play by the economic and welfare rules; to accept the national norms on such things as the role of religion in society and free speech, and the broad legal and political equality of women; and to speak the language well enough to take part in social and economic life.

But for any modern society to function well something more than this basic political and social 'hardware' is required – something that embraces the 'software', too, the felt reality of British life, norms and institutions. The software stressed by Gordon Brown and others is the glue of British values. But this often ends up sounding banal – 'Britishness is about tolerance and diversity' – moreover a focus on values implies that Britain has a monopoly on certain virtues. It is preferable to think in terms of British 'ideals', which are less given by history and more open to being shaped by today's citizens. John Denham, the influential Labour chair of the Home Affairs Select Committee, has talked about a twenty-first century British identity being 'created not discovered'. He is right that there is an element of 'nation-building' involved in giving new meaning to modern Britishness, but it is worth stressing that it is not being built out of thin air. Most of the raw material for its construction will still come from Britain's history and its ways of life.

In fact, rather than thinking about integration in terms of values, with all the vagueness and subjectivity that this entails, it is more useful to think in terms of a citizenship contract – a traditional political contract based on the 'vertical' state-based rights and duties (some of which are listed above) but also a social contract based on the 'horizontal' citizen-to-citizen solidarity embodied in the welfare state and our shared experiences of using common institutions, many with local roots, such as the NHS, schools, pubs, the BBC, public transport, sports and leisure centres, or more recently the Sure Start children's centres. Robert Hazell of the Constitution Unit has spoken usefully about the contract of national citizenship emerging out of the intersection of interests, institutions and ideals.

There is something else, too, something less instrumental that a progressive national citizenship should encourage in as many people as possible – a primary emotional commitment to this place and its people. As Bhikhu Parekh has written in *Prospect*:

Societies are not held together by common interest and justice alone. If they were, the sacrifices that their members make for each other including sharing resources and giving up their lives in wars and national emergencies would be inexplicable. They need emotional bonding . . . that in turn springs from a common sense of belonging, from the recognition of each other as members of a single community. And that requires a broadly shared sense of national identity – a sense of who they are, what binds them together and makes them members of this community rather than some other.[11]

This is all circular . waffle galore.

4. Different kinds of Britishness

Most of the things discussed above cannot be legislated for or even influenced by politics in any simple way – the national citizenship contract will remain largely (but not entirely) a political metaphor. Moreover, the contract even as a metaphor will have fuzzy edges and will change over time, sometimes quite rapidly. National identities evolve constantly, with or without immigration, as new generations emerge with different interests and priorities. But by stretching backwards and forwards in time, in some recognisable way, the national story also provides a reassuring framework for people's lives.

People often say that it is a good idea in theory to promote a stronger sense of national citizenship but in practice it is pointless because there is too little agreement about what Britishness means. Yet, as the previous chapter tries to show, the Britishness contract is not that complex or demanding and for most people it is just a description of what they already sign up to. Moreover, at a more subjective level there is surely no problem with different kinds of people expressing their membership of the British club in very different ways. A recent immigrant is likely to have a more abstract, rational identification with the country, with the opportunities it provides, with the laws and traditions that have made it a desirable place to live – and that identification may happily coexist with continuing commitments to a country of origin. A citizen from one of the long-established ethnic groups – the English in England or Scots-Protestants in Scotland – is likely to be more instinctively aware of a shared history, traditions and ways of life. There is no reason to think of either sense of being British as superior to the other. Many on the left are suspicious of the idea of an instinctive sense of national belonging, but this is invariably the form it takes for members of the majority in most countries and there is no reason why, especially in twenty-first-century Britain, the instinct should be a menacing one.

Of course, instinct alone is not enough; people also have to *learn* how to become citizens of a complex modern state whether their families have lived here for centuries or whether they are recent arrivals. A progressive civic nationalism is based on the fact that ethnicity and citizenship are not the same things and that it is possible to be a full and welcome citizen of Britain while belonging to a minority ethnic, racial or religious group. And here the habits of mind created by the British distinction between the state and its four constituent ethnic nations is a help not a hindrance. (The 2002 MORI poll for the Commission for Racial Equality,[12] which found that 86 per cent of British people do not think you have to be white to be truly British, is reassuring evidence that most people do not have a racial view of British citizenship. And no more than one-third of whites, of any class, think that you have to be white to be English, *British Social Attitudes* 2000.[13])

But equally there is nothing inherently illiberal about belonging to a majority ethnic group. People on the left, especially English people on the left, tend to be rather nervous about the idea of ethnicity – but an ethnicity is simply a group of people with loosely shared ancestry and common historical myths. The ethnically English, who probably still make up about 75 per cent of the population of England, include descendants of the Celts, Vikings, Normans, Huguenots, Jews, Irish, Africans, Indians and others who have intermarried over the centuries with the Anglo-Saxons who became the dominant group in England in the sixth century. Contrary to the hostile 'blood and soil' caricature of the left, Englishness has been a rather open ethnicity. And, increasingly, its symbols are being embraced by ethnic minority citizens, too (particularly in relation to sporting events), who were once said to feel comfortable only with the more political–legal category of Britishness. A stronger sense of Anglo-British national citizenship does not need to be, indeed cannot be, built against Englishness. Britain is a multinational democratic state inevitably dominated by the English, in the way that the Swiss-Germans dominate the Swiss federation or the Anglo-Canadians the Canadian federation.

'Multiculturalism has failed. Angles should learn to be Saxons.'

A progressive civic nationalism is not, to repeat, just a means to smooth the integration of new citizens, it is also a way of highlighting and sustaining a sense of common citizenship among long-established citizens. But by thinking more clearly about integrating outsiders, we are also forced to think more clearly about what we want them to integrate into. Over the past 40 years Britain has lost the ability to tell a clear story about itself and that is reflected in the indistinct sense of citizenship that many recent immigrants have acquired.

why?

> When in 2001 the Home Office floated the idea that a working knowledge of English might be necessary for those applying for citizenship the idea was dismissed as 'linguistic colonialism' by the chief executive of the Joint Council for the Welfare of Immigrants

complains Robert Colls.[14] And similarly in *Open Democracy* Tariq Modood said:

> We cannot both ask new Britons to integrate and to go around saying that being British is, thank goodness, a hollowed-out, meaningless project whose time has come. This will produce confusion and detract from the sociological and psychological processes of integration, as well as offering no defence against the calls of other loyalties and missions.[15]

Integration is, of course, a two-way process. The question is how far does each side in this process move. Sometimes in discussions on the left about migration there is an assumption that Britain must radically adapt its way of life or reach out to meet newcomers half way. This 'equality of adaptation' idea is disproportional, reflecting the British left's ambivalence about national feeling and its recent focus on minority grievance. Equality of adaptation does not in fact happen but the fear that it does is a source of great anxiety in middle Britain. Britons must adapt to the extent of treating any new group of citizens with fairness and dignity. And it is, of course, especially important that the state itself and key institutions like the police and the criminal justice system are strongly committed to the principle of equal citizenship. In the longer run as different ethnic groups grow in size and importance they will, willy nilly, change the host society (the point Robin Cook was making in his famous remark about chicken tikka masala being Britain's favourite dish). But in the nature of things most of the adaptation will, initially, be on the side of the newcomers who have chosen to live in an already existing society with established norms and traditions.

This does not mean assimilation. There is no need to abandon all ties to a country of origin or to fall in with every aspect of the British way of life; it is any case too varied to do so – the majority population is itself a collection of minorities. But it is important that newcomers acknowledge that Britain is not just a random collection of individuals; they are joining a society, which, although hard to describe, is real enough. It is not enough to point out, as many multiculturalists do, that there is no simple moral consensus in a country like Britain. Of course that is true. The political challenge is to create and sustain a minimum degree of moral consensus and solidarity in an otherwise highly pluralistic society. Diversity in itself is neither good nor bad, it is fairness that matters.

Clearly, a developed, liberal society such as Britain can and does sustain a huge variety of beliefs and lifestyles, all of which are compatible with an adequate sense of Britishness. We do not all have to like each other, or agree with each other or live like each other for the glue to work. As the philosopher David Miller has written:

> *Liberal states do not require their citizens to believe liberal principles, since they tolerate communists, anarchists, fascists and so forth. What they require is that citizens should conform to liberal principles in practice and accept as legitimate policies that are pursued in the name of such principles, while they are left free to advocate alternative arrangements. The same must apply to immigrant groups, who can legitimately be required to abandon practices that liberalism condemns, such as the oppression of women, intolerance of other faiths and so on.*[16]

Miller is right. Liberalism and pluralism (the belief that there can be many different conceptions of the good life within the same society) are normally close allies but when they conflict it is liberalism that must prevail. Or to put it another way a liberal state has the right to outlaw things that challenge its core assumptions – such as the emergence of separate legal–political enclaves that would be implied, for example, in the acceptance of Sharia law for Muslims in areas of high Muslim settlement.

NB.

When people assert that cultural pluralism and liberalism can conflict it is, indeed, usually Muslim minorities in the West that are being alluded to. Britain's Muslim minority of 1.5–2 million people is itself a highly varied group but between 60 and 70 per cent of British Muslims come from, or have parents who came from, Pakistan and Bangladesh (often from the rural parts of those countries) and it is among this group that the 'classical' problems of integration and social and economic failure are most starkly posed. Between mainstream Britain and much of the Pakistani and Bangladeshi minority there is a big divide in terms of wealth, education and cultural traditionalism. Moreover, integration is often complicated by modern communications (radio, television, internet) which make it easier to retain strong, permanent links with the country of origin and remain linguistically embedded in that world.

And now, thanks in part to the embattled global situation of Islam and recent British foreign policy, the question of divided loyalties is also raised more starkly for many Muslims than it is for most other immigrant groups. Some commentators argue that there is a special problem with integrating pious Muslims because of the very nature of Islam: the absence of a distinction between political and religious life; the traditionalism of the religion based on a literal reading of an unquestionable single text; and the fact that it is a proselytising, universalist religion that once dominated the world – and in the eyes of some Muslims should do so again.

It is probably true that there are more pious Muslims in Britain who are indifferent to – or even hostile to – the society around them than can be found in any other big minority.[17] Whether there is a 'special' problem with Islam or whether it is the usual problems of integration expressed in more acute form than with other big minorities is, for these purposes, an academic question. But as Ted Cantle's report into the 2001 race riots in northern England made clear there does seem to be a special problem of social distance and 'parallel lives' between the white working class and the Asian, mainly Muslim, minority in parts of northern England.[18]

Notwithstanding these problems there have actually been notable advances in the political standing of British Muslims since 1997: Muslim political representation has increased and Muslim preferences have prevailed on such things as faith schools and the religious hatred legislation. However, these advances are seldom acknowledged by the main Muslim organisations, which continue to focus relentlessly on 'Islamophobia' and appear to place most of the blame for the relative socioeconomic failure of the Muslim minority at the door of white society (despite the fact that other minorities – Hindus, Indians and the Chinese for example – do markedly better than whites in educational outcomes).

There may be a wider problem here of accommodating more religiously defined groups into modern Britain's sometimes aggressive secularism. As Tariq Modood has written:

> *While majority cultures are not homogeneous, there is indeed a growing mainstream that cuts across ethnicity and has an inclusive dynamic. This mainstream is individualistic, consumerist, materialist, and hedonistic, and is shaped by a globalising political economy, the media, and commercialised popular culture. This allows it to be pluralistic in terms of accommodating niche markets and lifestyle choices. . . . What it cannot accommodate so easily are minorities who as groups reject or are rejected by significant parts of this individualistically diverse mainstream.*[19]

The recent cartoon controversy raised very acutely this question of how far pious Muslims can expect to impose their religious prohibitions on a society which is dominated by the assumptions of liberal securalism. In my view Muslims will have to learn to turn a blind eye to material which mocks or satirises their faith, just as pious Christians have had to. Suspending the normal rules of free expression on behalf of the Muslim minority (in fact a minority of the minority) would be a clear example of a disproportional adaptation that risks contributing to majority resentment of all Muslims and also fails to challenge European Muslims with the necessity of accepting western liberal rules, at least in the public domain.

??

5. The welfare state and majority reassurance

The welfare state lies at the heart of a progressive civic nationalism. It is potentially both part of the problem and part of the solution from the point of view of sustaining solidarity in more individualistic and diverse societies.

It is potentially part of the problem when we consider whether it is possible to hold on to the level of sharing and redistribution at national level that grew out of the more intense sense of national membership 50 years ago. So far, that problem is only a distant rumble. The academic work of Robert Puttnam, Alberto Alesina, Stuart Soroka and others suggests that in America there is a negative trade-off between racial and ethnic diversity and levels of trust and welfare spending, especially (in the case of welfare spending) when members of minority ethnic groups are disproportionately concentrated among the poorest and most state-dependent citizens. But in Europe the size of the welfare state remains at historically high levels even as diversity of all kinds continues to rise. European welfare states certainly have powerful forces preserving them as they are. According to Peter Taylor-Gooby:

> *During the past 15 years, the periods of most rapid increase in social expenditure in Germany, the Netherlands and Italy have corresponded to periods when the foreign born population increased.*

. . . In the European context, an increase in the foreign-born population seems generally to coincide with rising rather than falling welfare state spending.[20]

But it would be complacent to consider this evidence decisive. The decline of solidarity is a slow, long-term process and over the next few decades several things – rising affluence and mobility, the ageing of the population, plus growing scepticism about the ability of the state to deliver – are all likely to increase resistance to paying high levels of taxation, especially when more of that tax may be going to groups with whom people sense little connection or fellow-feeling.

If the lack of fellow-feeling towards newer citizens is potentially part of the problem it is the actual contribution of such citizens that may be part of the solution. That contribution allows the focus to be placed on our commonality as taxpayers and users of public services and allows a positive case for moderate immigration on the grounds that it helps to shore up parts of the welfare state and cushions the adaptation to a society with an older average age. The first jobs that unskilled immigrants take are often at the lower end of the welfare economy (public or private). Some commentators go on to claim that immigration brings large fiscal benefits to Britain. The reality seems to be that the costs and benefits more or less balance each other out. According to John Salt and James Clarke of the migration research unit at UCL:

The one study of the fiscal effect for the UK estimated a net annual gain to the economy of £2.5 billion, but the authors admitted that in the absence of better data this could only be an approximation. Other authors have suggested the gain is much lower or non-existent. . . . And when the impact of migrants on the native workforce, particularly at the less-skilled end, is taken into account, the fiscal impact is more likely to be negative.[21]

In 'middle Britain' needing migrants for the service and welfare jobs that the existing population no longer wants to do is the single most persuasive case for immigration. But not everyone benefits from high levels of low-skill immigration – it means extra pressure on low-cost housing and public services as well as downward pressure on the wages of the less skilled. Mervyn King, governor of the Bank of England, said recently that the inflow of migrant labour, especially from eastern Europe, is an important factor in reducing inflationary pressure in the labour market.[22] Labour MPs from the more depressed corners of the high-immigration south east of England, such as Margaret Hodge, MP for Barking, are well aware of the negative impact this has had on their low income constituents. Jon Cruddas, MP for nearby Dagenham, wrote recently:

> For many of my constituents the value of their social wage is in decline. Public service improvements fail to match local population expansion. . . . And at work their terms and conditions are under threat as they compete for work with cheap immigrant labour.[23]

Cruddas also points out that only about one employer a year is prosecuted for employing illegal immigrant labour.

Moreover, alongside these 'objective' grounds for anxiety among lower income groups, high levels of mobility and immigration also tend to generate a more generalised 'subjective' anxiety that other people, especially newcomers, are unfairly jumping ahead of you in the queue of life and 'taking advantage' in some way. Recently the 'other' said to be taking advantage is likely to have been an asylum seeker; 20 years ago the culprit would most likely have been an indigenous single mother on benefit.

Clearly much of the disproportionate passion invoked against the other, and indeed the very identity of the other, is connected to media reporting. But it is not enough to say that people are suffering from *Daily Mail*-induced false consciousness. The form of this anxiety can perhaps be influenced by newspapers but the emotion itself seems to be deeply ingrained. Many poorer people in welfare states have an acute sensitivity to losing their place in the queue to 'free riders'. A 2004 *Prospect*/MORI poll[24] asked whether people felt that other people were taking unfair advantage in their use of public services and benefits, and 45 per cent of respondents said yes. The groups most commonly blamed for taking unfair advantage were asylum seekers and recent immigrants, but, more optimistically, the long-established minorities featured hardly at all, suggesting that given time people do extend their idea of the 'we' when it comes to sharing resources.

The sensitivity to free-riding is another element in the rising salience of security and identity issues. It seems to be connected to the opacity of developed urban societies and the fact that even people on low incomes pay large chunks of their income to the state but cannot clearly see how much of the money is coming back to them. It is true that more than half of all income tax is paid by the top 10 per cent of earners but people on low incomes pay a larger *proportion* of their incomes in tax, mainly indirect tax, than people on high incomes (the richest 20 per cent pay 35 per cent, the poorest 20 per cent pay 37.9 per cent). Even if they are net beneficiaries of the tax and welfare system people will still often object to public resources going to someone they do not regard as deserving – whether indigenous or not. (In racially polarised towns public spending can also easily create arguments about disproportionate public spending in one area or another as has been documented in the 2001 race riots in England's northern towns.)

Historically, immigrants to Britain received no public assistance because they arrived before the existence of the welfare state. That changed with postwar immigration; outsiders were now joining societies with a higher level of mutuality than in the past. In their recent book, *The New East End*, Geoff Dench, Kate Gavron and the late Michael Young[25] discovered deep unease among the white working class of east London about the shift from mutual forms of welfare to the modern state's needs-based system, which was thought to favour outsiders, particularly the Bangladeshi newcomers, who, it was felt, had not paid their way:

Establishing a common understanding of reciprocity is a difficult enough challenge within a group that has fixed membership, but it becomes increasingly important to sustain where newcomers are entering the group and need to be brought into a pre-existing moral economy and loop of mutual support.[26]

Moreover, in the case of the east end there was a historical dimension to this resentment:

The post-war compact was understood by working class east enders as admitting them to full membership of British society. To some extent this itself recognised historical debts by the nation to its lowest orders. A further compact made soon afterwards with colonial citizens, especially one not properly discussed within the nation in the way that the creation of the welfare state had been, was felt as a serious diminution, even a snatching back, of their own recent 'reward'.[27]

These widely held misgivings about welfare and immigration are partly based on prejudice (especially the free-rider anxieties I have labelled 'subjective') but they must still be answered, not just dismissed. And, above all, if the welfare 'contract' is to stand at the heart of national solidarity it is essential – more essential than in the past when Britain was a more closed society – to establish clearer and more transparent rules of national membership and citizenship entitlement (see chapter 6). Such rules make it easier to beat back the myths and exaggerations of populist political parties like the BNP.

Labour *has* responded to these popular anxieties by, among other things, stressing the 'something for something' conditionality of welfare for all citizens both long established and new. John Denham explained why in a *Prospect* essay describing an extended focus group in his Southampton constituency:

Fairness comes up in every important area of public policy: what happens at work; access to communal goods; the way public services are delivered. It's not a selfish 'I should get more' reaction, but something broader and more complex. Is good behaviour rewarded? Do I get a fair return for what I put in? Are some people getting something for nothing? There's a sense of fairness here – the belief that there is a set of obligations and opportunities that should underpin British society. When people say 'it's not fair', it is usually because they believe that the balance of duties and rewards – 'the fairness code' – has been upset. . . . The fairness code cuts across the values of left and right. Few people express the left's traditional concern about income equality . . . and there is little interest in the right's individualistic, self-reliant model of social and economic policy. . . . Public services should be for people who are entitled to them, need them, and use them responsibly.[28]

But there is a problem for those wishing to reassure Denham's constituents or Michael Young's east enders that the 'something for something' fairness code is working. The British welfare state has been drifting away from a contribution-based system (at least for unemployment benefit and pensions), with its link between what you put in and what you get out, to a system based on needs and residence-based entitlement, regardless of what you have paid in. To preserve popular support for such a 'common pool' welfare system you need to have some confidence in your fellow citizens to play by the rules and not to take advantage. But we have been making this shift to more common pool welfare at a time when general trust levels have been declining and when people believe that Britain no longer fully controls its borders and thus who becomes a fellow citizen. This latter belief is partly justified. As any migration expert will tell you it is hard to keep full control of your borders and remain an open society when there are 90 million journeys into and out of Britain each year.[29]

It is difficult to return to a more contribution-based welfare system because it discriminated against women who break their careers; nor do we want to turn Britain into a fortress. But what centre-left politics can and must do is help to neutralise the fears people have – both real and imaginary – about free-riding in more mobile and diverse societies. As a political realist I prefer measures of majority, and minority, reassurance (see the first two policy proposals in chapter 6), rather than exhortations to embrace diversity.

NB

6. Policy implications

A renewed sense of civic British nationalism cannot simply be commanded by well-meaning politicians. But Britishness is a big idea, bequeathed by history, that is baggy enough to allow today's politicians to fill it with at least some new meanings. It is a tall order to expect Britishness to provide a new sense of unity to the four nations which make up the postdevolution UK, to act as a substitute for the decline of local communities, and to encapsulate a more generous notion of the collective 'we' – allowing for moderate levels of immigration, high levels of welfare and better integration of both old and new citizens. But below are some suggestions about how a civic British nationalism might do *some* of that work, especially for the English. Some are specific policy ideas, others looser assumptions that should underpin policy thinking or political rhetoric. Few of them are original: the first two sections are largely defensive, reassurance measures; the subsequent three point towards a more positive 'nation building' ethos for today's Britain. (It is worth noting that several of the ideas are borrowed from the practice of countries such as Canada and Sweden, which are usually seen as being in the progressive vanguard on these issues.)

Immigration, citizenship and integration
Immigration brings benefits and costs; neither are evenly distributed.

Mass immigration is not popular. But historically high levels of 150,000-plus net incomers a year are likely to continue for a couple of decades primarily for reasons of economic demand, but also because of family reunion and asylum.[30]

The Labour government's twin-track approach of trying to win political support for immigration while also reassuring people that the flow is properly controlled in the interests of existing citizens strikes the right balance. To that end the government is trying to reduce illegal and lower-skill immigration (through a points system). That requires controlling and counting what is actually happening at our borders, eventually through electronic embarkation controls tied to a national identity card system, so we have a better idea of who is coming into and leaving the country (work on this is already under way). Political symbolism is also important here. The government should produce a detailed but readable annual 'migration report' on what we know about those leaving and coming to the country. The reports should be produced by an independent migration panel. This panel should have representatives of all the main political parties, employers and unions, immigrant groups, academic researchers and so on. The object is to make the migration debate as transparent and non-partisan as possible and to communicate the idea that we are in control of who becomes a fellow citizen. The migration panel and its research team might form the core of a new 'migration and integration' Whitehall department. It is often argued that the Home Office is too large and covers too many high-profile sensitive policy areas and is thus prone to knee-jerk initiatives.

Despite majority (and minority) scepticism about high levels of immigration, people are usually happy enough to accept newcomers both nationally and locally when they are seen to contribute and do not cut themselves off from the mainstream. An informal assumption – the migration equivalent of John Rawls's difference principle on income inequality – might apply here, with migration welcomed to the extent that it can be shown to improve the lives of the least well-off British citizens. That will always be difficult to prove conclusively but government and employers should certainly do more to show that they are doing all they can to get *existing* citizens into jobs and training before reaching for immigration as the short-termist answer to labour and skill shortages (unemployment in London is still over 7 per cent, much of it concentrated among ethnic minorities, and there are more than two million people on incapacity benefit, many of whom would like to work). The dilemma for the left here is that its internationalism conflicts with its support for equality at home. Its internationalism requires the most open possible door to immigrants, especially from poor countries, but a high level of unskilled migration depresses wages and is bad for domestic equality.

No!₂

Making citizenship more visible (citizenship ceremonies and oaths of allegiance, citizenship classes in schools) and raising, somewhat, the qualification hurdles (such as language and citizenship tests) is belatedly bringing Britain into line with much of the rest of the developed world, including the United States. At present permanently resident non-citizens have almost all the benefits of citizenship except for being able to vote or serve on juries. More benefits, especially long-term benefits such as pensions, should be based on *citizenship* rather than merely *residence*. Indeed, we should consider establishing a more formal two-tier citizenship, a temporary British resident status with fewer rights and duties for those who want to come here to work for a few years and then return home, alongside a more formal, full citizenship. (The recent RSA migration report suggests offering some workers from outside the EU a five-year visa which would entitle them to work but not to bring their families.[31]) There are complex issues relating to welfare access but it should be possible to work out a system which would be of benefit both to Britain and to the temporary worker, and would help to underline the 'specialness' of full citizenship. A system of full and temporary citizenship in Britain would need to take care that members of the settled minorities did not feel lumped together with temporary citizens in a 'second class' box. But survey evidence suggests that people do make a distinction between, for example, members of the settled Afro-Caribbean and Asian minorities, who are considered fully British, and asylum seekers or temporary workers (often whites from eastern Europe) who are not.

metics

Outsiders are not *entitled* to British citizenship. For those new migrants who do become full British citizens it is important for the rest of us to have confidence in them and to feel that they have 'worked their passage', have earned their citizenship through a phased entitlement to its benefits. One simple way of highlighting this earned citizenship would be to follow the Canadian model and adopt a more overt five-year probationary period for citizenship, during which time you would not qualify for full political and welfare rights. There is in fact such a probationary period in Britain but it needs greater visibility. At the end of the probationary period if you have not committed a crime above a certain level of seriousness and have passed your language and citizenship tests – with free lessons for both – you would be welcomed into full citizenship. To draw greater attention to citizenship ceremonies it might be a good idea to follow the practice of places such as Canada and hold as many as possible during a specially designated citizenship week.

The overall integration picture in Europe is not as bad as events such as the 7/7 bombs and the French suburban riots make it appear. But Europe's political classes face rather similar problems of *Aha!* simultaneously reassuring majority populations – in particular the white working class – that they will not be disadvantaged by large-scale immigration, while trying to make real the offer of equal citizenship both to new citizens and to members of the settled ethnic minority communities. Notwithstanding today's equality and anti-discrimination legislation the creation of 'felt' equality of citizenship for minorities in Britain and elsewhere has proved more elusive than expected, at least for some groups. This may be partly the fault of unrealistic expectations created by the liberal 'blank sheet' fallacy of human affiliation. Moreover, equality of citizenship (legally, politically and socially, though not, of course, economically) is a very recent thing in human history and not even truly realised among the indigenous majority. Yet the larger numbers and greater confidence of second and third generation immigrants means that any falling short of the ideal of both formal and felt equality is often met with expressions of angry disappointment. That disappointment, sometimes accompanied by demands for special treatment and extra resources, can trigger a hostile reaction from the majority, especially 'left-behind' groups, leading to a spiral of mutual resentment.

The recent history of colonialism may also play a role in exacerbating this integration problem, especially with Muslim minorities in Britain and in France. In the first wave of postwar immigration the colonial connection was usually seen as an advantage on both sides, thanks to the institutional and linguistic familiarity between migrant and host community. But in subsequent generations the failure to achieve full, felt equality may be attributed – and sometimes rightly – to a mix of fear, guilt and mutual resentment on the part of the descendants of the colonisers and the colonised.

Successful integration is not easily amenable to public policy; and as far as it is amenable it will mean very different things in a big city with a 30–40 per cent ethnic minority population, a suburb with a 10 per cent ethnic minority population and a market town with a 1 per cent ethnic minority population. And it will also mean very different things for an educated migrant raised in a broadly western way compared with someone raised in rural poverty with a traditional worldview. Much integration takes place spontaneously in private life – away from the promptings of the local or national state. In the middle-class suburbs and professional and business life it is often a reasonably smooth and unremarkable process. But it does not always happen spontaneously or quickly; often it has to be learnt and nurtured. And it is worth considering what role public policy can play here. Public integration measures can be usefully subdivided into three categories.

First, 'rites of passage' – citizenship ceremonies, language tests, probationary periods, the teaching of citizenship in schools to all young people – are designed to impress on both new citizens and long-standing ones that they are joining, or are already part of, something of significance that is highly valued. (Another ceremony should be added to this list for *all* citizens: a ceremony at the registering of a child's birth. This ceremony, and an accompanying booklet, should explain what is expected of good parents but also what parents can expect of the state in terms of childcare, education and health services.)

Second, public authorities should provide positive incentives to mix. Some ethnic or religious groups prefer to congregate among themselves but public authorities should operate a rule of thumb in which they try to ensure a high degree of trust-building contact in at least one important area of life: housing, work, schooling, sports and leisure and so on. In the heyday of multiculturalism in the 1980s and 1990s too much public money was spent in a manner that had the effect of encouraging and perpetuating separation. Public money would be better spent encouraging organisations that bring different groups into contact. As one small example, the Commission for Racial Equality has just been given £3 million by the government to encourage black and Asian cricket and football teams to start playing white teams rather than only other black and Asian teams.

Third, public authorities should provide *dis*incentives to separate. This should include clear national norms on religious clothing in public places – for example, yes to the *hijab* but no to the *burkha* in schools, public offices and so on, with its complete screening away of the woman from her fellow citizens. And, more controversially, it should mean support for David Blunkett's plea to the south Asian community to find spouses from within their community here, rather than returning to the subcontinent for them. The latter practice can short-circuit the process of integration by bringing in spouses who are often completely new to Britain's norms and language. It is not appropriate for a liberal society to interfere directly in the marriage choices of its citizens, but it is appropriate for a liberal society to control who becomes a citizen: language and citizenship tests for spouses and raising the minimum age qualification could help to reduce the negative impact on integration. Clearly, in both the second and third categories above the state is often attempting to direct people away from their freely taken choices which may well create resentment. But encouraging integration is often an inherently illiberal process; there is, at least, a difficult balancing act between the public good and individual choice.

Welfare

Generous welfare and thriving public services could be victims of a fragmenting society; they could also form a rallying point for a society seeking new sources of cohesion. If popular support for immigration requires a clearer and more overt contract between new citizens and the host society, a thriving welfare state requires a more overt contract between all citizens and society. If we want people to continue paying more than one-third of their income to the state, universalism is usually preferable to means-testing and the visible conditionality of entitlements is essential. Citizens need to believe that the vast majority of people are playing by John Denham's national 'fairness code'.[32] Where possible, benefits should be (as they often already are) conditional on appropriate behaviour, such as the commitment to genuinely seek a job in return for unemployment benefit. And there should be a policy bias towards re-establishing a social insurance connection with welfare payments wherever possible, especially for long-term benefits such as pensions.

Britain has an unusually open labour market by European standards, which has been helpful for minority integration (unemployment levels are higher among ethnic minority Britons than white Britons but are much lower than they are for minorities in France or Germany). But Britain also has an unusually open welfare system. Almost anyone, including visitors and illegal immigrants, can access public education and healthcare if they have an address. In a more mobile society such openness is no longer feasible, especially when public spending is being squeezed. By connecting your entitlement to your citizenship status, ID cards would go some way to ensuring the fairness code is not breached and would help to dampen free-rider anxieties. Identity cards are also a badge of Britishness which transcend our more particular regional, ethnic or racial identities. John Denham again:

> Nothing is more damaging to social cohesion than the belief that expensive tax-funded services are too readily available to people who are not entitled to them. The legal basis for access to the NHS and

education is not clear enough for a modern mobile world; this is unsustainable given our record investments in these services. Citizens must be sure that access to public services is not a free-for-all but is based on a protected entitlement. Identity cards . . . will demonstrate a commitment to using taxpayers' money fairly.[33]

If over the next few years a way is found to return more power and control of public money, including welfare payments, to more local bodies that should, in theory, make welfare solidarities more visible and less susceptible to free-rider anxieties. (This can work the other way, too; it was the very visibility of public money being channelled towards different ethnic groups in the divided northern mill towns that was one factor behind the 2001 riots.) Even if power is not substantially devolved there are many small institutional reforms that could help to increase neighbourliness and social mixing. For example, with greater mobility and the decline of extended families people in big cities are less likely to know older and vulnerable people living nearby who could benefit from assistance from time to time. A national telephone and internet volunteering network – designed to put local supply in touch with local demand – could help to compensate for that lack of local knowledge. The mentoring of recent immigrants and asylum seekers could be part of the same network. Such a national body need not compete with existing private voluntary bodies but a national brand (plus a widely advertised website and/or telephone number) could act as an umbrella for existing voluntary organisations.

Another small change to the way in which the state provides social security and employment services could act as a local reinforcement of community. If 'one-stop' community and welfare offices – as well as providing employment and social security services – could also include a high-quality, free, advisory function on everything from pensions to a healthy diet – a sort of free *Which?* magazine service – it would attract a far more socially mixed group of users and act as a focus for local activities. With the use of the internet this public advice function could be both sophisticated and cheap; local staff (or volunteers) could access the latest advice on, say, pensions from a central panel of government experts and pass it on to enquirers.

Education

As society becomes more diverse and more affluent, our sharing of common spaces and institutions dwindles. Those public institutions that we do still share, such as education and health services, become more important. The school also becomes a key institution of integration, especially for the children of recent migrants and especially when they may be segregated, often by choice, in most other areas of their life – housing, religious worship and so on. Curriculums should reflect the distinct background of pupils when a school draws many pupils from the same immigrant group but British national history and literature – and more recently British citizenship – should be a central part of every schoolchild's education (instead of black history month, why not black British history month?). The history of this island should be taught as an over-arching story from the stone age to the swinging sixties, as the story of France is taught in French schools. There is, of course, a place for more thematic history, too, but surely the first year of secondary school is a time to get the basic framework of British history understood.

The teaching of citizenship in schools has, by all accounts, been rather patchy so far. It might work better if it were integrated into the teaching of history – there is after all a Whiggish story to be told from the Magna Carta to the race discrimination laws about the gradual extension of citizenship rights. And the history of empire – taught as objectively as possible, not as a morality tale of good or evil – should also be part of the compulsory curriculum, thereby binding together the historical fates of both the British majority and many postwar immigrants. It is now possible to pass through secondary school without learning the outline of the national story, something that would be unthinkable in most other countries. At a time of rapid change people want a sense of roots and history is one way of providing it.

Also, if common schooling is important in fostering trust and understanding across ethnic and religious divides then surely there should be a policy bias against faith schools, although it is clearly hard to abolish existing faith schools and then unfair not to allow Muslim ones. (There should at least be a single national religious education curriculum which applies to faith schools too.) Not all faith schools are mono-ethnic: Christian ones in many areas are ethnically mixed. But with or without a big expansion in faith schools ethnic residential segregation is likely to mean a growing number of schools dominated by one ethnic group. In areas where there are many such schools some effort should be made to make sure that different schools with markedly different ethnic compositions come together in twinning schemes to share certain activities or resources. It would also have a positive impact on both non-white and white pupils if there were more ethnic minority teachers; currently one-sixth of state school pupils come from ethnic minority backgrounds but only one-eleventh of teachers.

As many minority groups are now over-represented in higher education – including Muslims, with half of all young Muslims now going to college – it will surely be only a matter of time before the minority teaching population rises. And higher education is currently one of the most effective ethnic melting-pots in British society (although there are also fears of ethnic minority concentration in lower status universities). This is another good reason for continuing the expansion of the university sector, notwithstanding all the difficulties and compromises it involves.

It is also worth exploring the idea of some kind of national citizenship service for school leavers, deliberately mixing up people from different social classes and ethnic backgrounds. If it is compulsory and if it involves young people leaving home for at least some of the service it will be expensive, but it is a price worth paying to create more common experiences across the social and ethnic divides. And there is no need to stop at school leavers – why not a civilian equivalent of the Territorial Army, whose members would be trained to help the emergency services in large-scale disasters? Such a civilian 'militia' might not be paid in the conventional manner but the civic contribution of members could be recognised with various perks from the state.[34]

The European Union

There is no reason why strong feelings of Britishness (and Englishness) cannot coexist with outward-looking international commitments, support for the pooling of national sovereignty and enthusiastic participation in bodies such as the EU. Other countries such as France combine both a stronger sense of national identity and a stronger historic commitment to the EU than Britain. Moreover the national interest argument for Europe is more persuasive now than it was in 1973 when we joined. Since enlargement to an EU of 25, the federalist argument has been defeated and the organisation is far less dominated by France and Germany. And while the EU does require the pooling of some sovereignty, the main issues in British politics – tax and spend, health, education, crime, personal tax levels, asylum and immigration – all remain overwhelmingly national matters.

One reason for British hostility to Europe is that both sides of the debate – Europhile and Eurosceptic – have had an interest in exaggerating the extent of European involvement in national life. However, another reason for Britain's relative lack of enthusiasm for Europe is that compared with many other European countries the British national identity has been more bound up with our political institutions and those institutions are, unavoidably, subject to some change and reform from Brussels. Other big European countries, by contrast, express their national identities more through language and way of life, making them less sensitive to change directed from Brussels. This, however, seems to be changing. As the importance of politics in general and parliament in particular recedes in our national life and Britons, too, come to express a more 'cultural' understanding of their identity, this problem with Europe may become less significant. And, at the same time, with the fading of the integrationist logic of the EU and Britain's greater influence in the institution, it should come to be seen as a less alien imposition.

But the EU does remain unavoidably complex. Greater familiarity could hardly breed greater contempt than already exists, so some sort of EU dimension ought to be added to citizenship classes to try to give people a better framework of understanding. A greater connection between national parliaments and EU decision-making would also help to make the EU less alien. Last year's failed EU Constitutional Treaty recommended better scrutiny of EU legislation by national parliaments and also proposed a sensible 'yellow card' system under which if a certain number of national parliaments agree that an EU measure is contrary to subsidiarity it must be looked at again. Another idea worth pursuing, proposed by the Centre for European Reform, is that each national EU commissioner should report once a year to his or her national parliament. *Nothing about controversy European parliament*

Symbols of Britishness

As we have seen, the idea of Britishness is currently becoming weaker not stronger, thanks in part to devolution. Old sources of loyalty and identity are in retreat – although we can see their continuing power in events such as the Queen Mother's funeral, the huge audiences for television programmes on British history and the continuing importance of Remembrance Day. But if younger generations can no longer see the point of the assumptions and conventions of the old Britishness – many of them forged in wartime or the days of empire – then we need the political imagination to create new ones, to help in the reshaping of a civic British national mythology. Symbols are important both for integrating outsiders and for validating the identity of the majority population. *This is all about conjuring!*

For the dominant English, as for the other nations of Britain, the idea of Britain is already a displacement, something with only 300 years of history and tradition to support it. But it makes sense to try to inject some new life into it. Britain does not have a national day; we should inaugurate one as Gordon Brown has suggested (and why doesn't he rename the Bank of England the Bank of Britain?). Such a national day might include a US-style state of the nation address delivered by the prime minister, instead of the rather technical, legislation-based Queen's speech, and it should be a focal point for citizenship ceremonies. It should be named 'British liberty' day to celebrate the post-1689 Whiggish liberal British culture of constitutionalism, rights and commerce. (The empire, for good and ill, was part of that story but, arguably, an aberration that lasted in its mature form only about 100 years.) The British national myth is of brave islanders defending freedom against domestic tyrants and continental conquerors. The British did not invent liberal civilisation – it was invented in northern Italy and the Netherlands and then transplanted to Britain – but we did pass it on to the rest of the world and, in 1940, stopped it from dying in Europe.

There are two big events coming up over the next decade or so – the Olympic Games in 2012 and the next coronation – both of which will provide an important focus to revive and revise the symbols of Britishness. The monarchy may be a fraying institution but it still registers strong support across ethnic and faith boundaries and, along with the army, has a strongly *British* identity. And without abandoning the ceremony and traditionalism which is a large part of the point of the monarchy it should still be possible to adapt it to reflect a renewed Britishness (a new coronation oath for example). The national flag and anthem remain central symbols of Britishness, and particularly in the case of the flag have become more so in the past few years. Sport is increasingly important both for English and British commitments. One of the most uplifting things about the 2004 Athens Olympic Games was seeing medal winners from Britain's ethnic minorities embracing the flag and talking about their pride in winning for their country. The run-up to the 2012 Olympics in London and the games themselves will provide a stage on which to reinforce the evolving symbolism of Britain's multiethnic national identity. (And before 2012, might we adopt a more inspiring national anthem?)

7. Conclusion

The idea that the essence of Britishness is its lack of an essence is in many ways an attractive one. Geography and history have bequeathed us strong liberal and individualist traditions – Britons (or at least the English majority) tend to regard the state as a necessary evil rather than a benign parent. And we are notoriously a private people rather uncomfortable with the idea of national solidarity or trying to legislate for something as intangible as 'social cohesion'. David Cameron is right to say that 'we don't do flags on our front lawns'. But to leave it at that is no longer sufficient. The fuzziness of our idea of national citizenship over recent decades threatens to disarm progressive politics in the face of a fragmenting common culture and the resurgence of security and identity issues. As Salman Rushdie wrote recently: 'No society, no matter how tolerant, can expect to thrive if its citizens don't prize what their citizenship means.'[35] Moreover, such a society will have no answer to the illiberal, populist politics that will flourish if not challenged by a realistic alternative. Populists present 'the people' as a homogeneous entity facing a closed, corrupt elite that has betrayed the interests of the long-suffering majority. Many of the policy points I have sketched in this pamphlet are defensive measures designed to persuade an anxious public that populists do not in fact have the answers and that British citizenship, membership of the British national community, remains valued and protected by mainstream politics.

A moderately strong state is a necessity in a technologically complex, highly urbanised society. But a generous welfare state, redistribution of wealth and a strong bond of citizenship are not necessary – and are in fact threatened by affluence, diversity, individualism and a creeping Americanisation. (The only possible countervailing factor that may benefit egalitarianism and solidarity, in the medium term, is some sort of energy rationing or household carbon emission limit.) Strenuous political efforts will be required merely to hold on to the welfare state as it is and enlightened self-interest is likely to be too thin a basis for it; some sense of fellow-feeling and shared collective destiny is necessary too. The nation state, the idea of a national story and the very idea of the British people, have all been in retreat in recent years. But the nation state remains the only feasible site for the sharing and redistribution of resources and it is therefore particularly in the interests of the centre-left to preserve it and help to fashion its evolution. Some redistribution does take place at the European level, and even the global level, but the sums are trivial and are unlikely to grow significantly precisely because there is not a strong sense of community at the European or global level.

Some of the measures discussed in this paper are aimed indirectly at a less tangible objective – how to deal with majority needs for belonging. We tend to think about culture and identity issues as something that relates only to minorities, what Eric Kaufmann has called 'asymmetrical multiculturalism'.[36] But perhaps the biggest question of all in modern Europe is how can majorities express their local and national identities without alienating minorities? How can outsiders be made to feel at home without making insiders feel that they have become strangers in their own home? It may no longer be enough to say that the prevailing culture already reflects that of the majority and thus provides sufficient meaning and sense of belonging to members of majority ethnic groups. An increasing number of people evidently do not feel this to be the case any longer. Multiethnic societies will not work by trying to suppress the history and identity of the majority ethnic group but rather by erecting a civic nationalist roof of political and social practices and institutions that all people – majority and minority – are committed to. The materials used in the construction of that roof will come mainly, but not exclusively, from the historic experience of the majority. But that is unavoidable: this is Britain, it is not anywhere.

The British state must, of course, strive to treat all its citizens equally. What is also required is a new vocabulary that can acknowledge real affinities of people and place and respect the feelings and traditions of Britain's historic, majority communities as well as its more recent minorities. At present there is a large conceptual and linguistic blank space between racism, at one end, and cosmopolitanism, at the other. Most people reside in this middle space but it is empty of words for us to describe our feelings and attitudes. The distinction between legitimate anxieties about migration-led social change and racism is not always easy to draw, but not to attempt to draw it at all or to collapse the two into each other is enormously damaging, especially for a centre-left politics that should be representing the interests of low-income citizens of all races and ethnicities. As Ted Cantle wrote in *The End of Parallel Lives?*:

> *Concerns about migration should not simply be dismissed as 'racist'.*
> *. . . We recognize that inward migration does create tensions. . . .*
> *Many disadvantaged communities will perceive that newcomers are*
> *in competition for scarce resources and public services . . . housing,*
> *education, health and other services all take time to expand. But*
> *people also take time to adjust. The identity of the host community*
> *will be challenged and people need sufficient time to come to terms*
> *with, and accommodate, incoming groups, regardless of ethnic*
> *origin. The pace of change . . . is simply too great in some areas at*
> *present.*[37]

The big question to be tested over the next 50 years or so is this: do you need a reasonably stable majority population, perhaps even a dominant culture, to generate the kind of political and welfare structures we associate with the European social model? The USA is a collection of minorities (the founding white Anglo-Saxon Protestants make up less than one-fifth of the total) which seems to reinforce the effects of an individualistic culture with low levels of social solidarity. As the majorities in Britain and other European societies start to shrink in size, a politics of progressive civic nationalism which provides that all-important political canopy over the thicker and more closed identities of ethnicity, religion and so on is surely the best means of holding on to the European social model – and of supplementing or even eventually replacing the glue of ethnicity with an ideology of civic national solidarity. If we cannot sustain that model, society will not fall apart, it will just gradually become less open, less equal, more violent and more socially and racially Balkanised.

The glue of national solidarity has in the past come more easily to those continental European states that had popular, national movements establishing the modern state through founding myths of struggle and written constitutions. Although this nationalism was partly discredited by the violence of the first part of the twentieth century it retains a popular and progressive legitimacy – a discourse of progressive nationalism comes quite naturally, say, to the French or Italian left in a way that it does not to the British left. Indeed, it could be argued that Britain has never had a fully 'national' stage in its modern history moving from an imperial sense of itself to a postnational one in one bound, leaving the political class – especially the left of centre part of it – with an unusually hostile attitude towards national feeling (something George Orwell enjoyed mocking). We may now be reaching the end of this British exceptionalism, and shifting towards a kind of 'national republicanism with British characteristics' (such as a constitutional monarch, a strong stress on individual liberty, suspicion of the state, and an unusual openness to the outside world). Such a refashioned, civic nationalism is the best means of appealing to a strong, generous notion of British citizenship – and may be the only feasible resting place for those ideas and values still associated with the political left.

8. Responses to David Goodhart's essay

Neal Ascherson

When David Goodhart wrote his famous 'Too diverse?' essay in *Prospect* two years ago,[38] he probably had little idea of the impact it would create. But it arrived at exactly the right moment, especially for those who claimed to detest what they thought it stood for.

The media, academia and the party-political world, all in their different ways, had been discussing obsessively the questions of immigration, asylum seekers and 'Islamic fundamentalism'. Could British society absorb all this? It was easy to find voices to say that it could or should, or that even to associate these topics was 'inappropriate'. But few people could be found to argue convincingly the other way. Then Goodhart's article suddenly produced the missing member of the cast: a commentator who was not a BNP thug or racist, but who – from an intellectual, even liberal point of view – argued that multiculturalism in Britain was failing.

His position was exaggerated out of recognition. It must have hurt Goodhart to be repeatedly put up in media cockfights as a spokesman against immigration (which he was not), or interviewed as if he were Britain's answer to Pim Fortuyn ('No more room for foreigners'). None the less, he became a familiar figure on the 'multiculturalism' conference circuit, endlessly trying to explain that he was concerned with threats to social solidarity, not with lurid scenarios of ethnic swamping and terrorism.

Goodhart's conversations with his critics, in or out of conference halls, seem to have persuaded him that his views needed to be refined, or at least expressed in a longer, more reasoned way. This pamphlet is the result. It's seriously and closely argued, and a lot of it is new. The underlying ideas, however, are the same. And I still have the same problems with them.

Crudely, his core proposition goes like this: more and more people from non-European cultures, especially Muslim ones, are entering Britain. The British majority considers, rightly or more often wrongly, that these incomers make little effort to integrate, that they debase wage levels and that they are in general 'free riders' on social benefits. These grievances are leading the majority to conclude that the postwar social compact – the welfare state in return for loyalty, work and taxes – has been violated. With public confidence withdrawn, the welfare state will then collapse.

Goodhart's remedy is to create, by several means, what he calls a new 'inclusive, progressive, civic British nationalism'. He proposes 'an overt political rhetoric of British national identity and solidarity – it provides a kind of over-arching "roof" under which the other more particular identities . . . can shelter'.

So much for the summary. For me, two immediate questions arise. The first one is about Goodhart's assertion that disgust with immigrants is leading the 'indigenous' British public to reject the welfare state. But is it? Where is the evidence that this is happening?

Xenophobic resentment, an old story in this country, can lead to all kinds of unrest from schoolyard bullying to riots. It can lead to furious protests, when hard-pressed families – in Glasgow for instance – ask why Kurds and Bosnians are given apartments when their own relations have been waiting to be re-housed for years. But that is protest against a city housing department, not against the whole benefit system. Heaven knows, there are many worse threats to the survival of the welfare state, financial and ideological. What grounds are there to say that the biggest threat is popular resentment against its supposed abuse by Asian or African immigrants?

My second problem is with the 'reinvent Britishness' therapy. This is a song sung in harmony with Gordon Brown's recent speeches on the subject. 'Islamic extremism . . . has . . . given a fresh impetus to careful thinking about how to foster a renewed sense of Britishness,' Goodhart writes, and a little later: 'Reviving the idea of Britishness is easier said than done.'

So why do it? What are we talking about? At one point, Goodhart says very plainly: 'Britain is (technically) not a nation at all but a state.' That would be fine if he stuck to it. But the very next paragraph begins: 'If British national citizenship is to be made more attractive . . .' and soon we get the first of many references to 'British national identity'. It isn't pedantry to say that this typically English confusion between nation and state fogs up the whole booklet.

Goodhart could have constructed his argument around a state or around a nation, but not around some shape-shifting chimera which is both at once. One option would have been to make his case for the nation of England, which is anyway the country he is talking about. He himself points out that the sense of 'British identity' is in retreat, most strikingly in Scotland but also in England where 'a limited revival of interest in Englishness' is under way. If so, then it would have made more sense to build a new sense of 'progressive nationalism' around Englishness, which is at least solidly rooted, and growing rather than declining. (It would also have been an act of enlightened courage. Why do English 'bourgeois liberals', the natural carriers of nationalist ideology, leave the shaping of this new English nationalism to fascists, hooligans and idiots?)

The other alternative, which would also have been lucid, would have been to make the state the clear and exclusive subject. How about 'reviving the idea of British statehood'? The state, after all, is an institution which does not confer identity but does award citizenship and its privileges, which for the last century at least has been in charge of redistributing wealth in the name of 'fairness' if not exactly equality, and which has accepted a responsibility for protecting the weak against the excesses of free-market capitalism owned by the strong.

Here, at least, a diminishing 'Britishness' does survive, not in cultures or ethnic identities but in a certain idea of what government is for. Gordon Brown was impressive when – before he began to talk about putting out more flags and instituting a British National Day – he said that patriotism should be about pride in the National Health Service. It follows that 'reconstructing Britishness' should mean reviving and expanding the role of the social-democratic state, returning to the ideals of fairness supported by government intervention which made the welfare state possible in the first place. But of course the whole current of politics now runs against this. Blairism has carried steadily forwards Thatcher's drive to evacuate the state from social and economic life. If there is a crisis of Britishness, it is because the British state does so much less for its subjects than it did before. It is simply far less present in people's lives.

Finally, I am not sure what David Goodhart wants to happen next. He is unhappy with the 1990s' model of 'multiculturalism', in which minorities were encouraged to entrench and celebrate their distinctiveness without any obligation to share the culture of the majority. Rightly, Goodhart sees that multiculturalism is not a destination but only a way-station on a journey of social change. But what comes after it? He would like to see more 'integration', to create a 'felt equality' of citizenship. This would be achieved by many kinds of measure: Goodhart wants citizenship, with full political and welfare rights, to be conditional on a probationary period in which the applicant commits no serious crimes and passes language and citizenship tests. There should be 'rites of passage' (ceremonies when full citizenship is granted or at the registering of a birth), 'incentives to mix' (to be enforced by public authorities in housing, schooling, sport and so on) and 'disincentives to separate' (for example, 'yes to the *hijab* but no to the *burkha* in schools [and] public offices . . . support for David Blunkett's plea to the south Asian community to find spouses from within their community here, rather than returning to the subcontinent for them'). Goodhart wants 'a single national religious educational curriculum which applies to faith schools too' and a single history curriculum in which 'the history of this island should be taught as an over-arching story from the stone age to the swinging sixties . . . a Whiggish story to be told from the Magna Carta to the race discrimination laws or the gradual extension of citizenship rights'.

Goodhart calls this 'integration'. To me, it sounds more like assimilation. He is describing a one-way process, in which the minority is persuaded by carrot and stick to adopt the culture of the majority in order to qualify for the rights of citizenship. But this does not recognise the reality of what is already happening on the ground in Britain's big cities. The next way-station after multiculturalism is not assimilation but hybridity.

The streets of London already show the beginnings of a two-way process in which both majority and minority are changing each other. They are evolving a fresh social synthesis which is neither a bouquet of contrasting cultures nor the adoption of the patterns of the old indigenous majority. Its sources include the spreading human rights culture, the withering away of careers in favour of short-term job opportunities, sex and marriage across old ethnic boundaries, sport and music and simply the 'hanging-out' habit which has renewed street life. Its take on 'Englishness' or state loyalty or civic duty is eclectic, opportunistic, unpredictable.

Hybridity brings new problems. Perhaps the most interesting is that it widens the cultural gap between town and country, between the hybrid cosmopolis and the hinterland of small towns and villages which often remain almost mono-ethnic – an intensely political question for the future. But hybridity is here to stay. It means, as Tom Nairn has written, 'the acceptance of irrevocable mixture as starting-point, rather than as a problem'.[39] I feel that David Goodhart's approach, at a deep level, is a romantic attempt to recall the irrevocable, to unscramble this omelette. Better to eat it and enjoy it.

Neal Ascherson, born in Edinburgh, is a journalist and writer who has worked mostly for the Observer *and the* Scotsman. *His most recent book is* Stone Voices: The search for Scotland *(Granta, 2003).*

David Blunkett

I welcome very strongly many of the themes outlined in David Goodhart's essay.

In *Politics and Progress* I wrote about 'civic republicanism';[40] here David Goodhart picks up this theme in relation to modern national sentiment and a view of progressive politics which addresses the crucial issues of identity and belonging.

In this pamphlet he also returns to some of the themes which will be familiar to those who read the original nationality and immigration white paper in February 2002,[41] published at the time that the far right was gaining momentum in France, the Netherlands and beyond. It laid out for the first time a nationality and immigration programme, rather than just an asylum programme, and included citizenship and identity as key themes.

The language in turn is very familiar to me, although I had to smile at the term 'the Home Office proposed'. The Home Office never proposed anything, it was ministers!

What is new, however, is the way in which David Goodhart reflects on the concept of the insider/outsider – the defence against the outlander – a recurring trait in all human groups. Putting it in these terms encourages us to think of this slightly differently and does help to explain the challenges often faced in achieving a welcome for newcomers even when they patently bring economic gains and increased prosperity.

The themes he raises – security and stability – are familiar ones. Globalisation and rapid change, reinforced as they were after the 11 September attack on the United States, require an understanding of the need for certainty, for roots and identity.

He is right: the progressive left in politics has always been suspicious of any form of homogeneity constructed from national pride. Strange, because the 'melting pot', which over the last 150 years has constituted the United States, has held together because of the reinforcement of a sense of national pride and therefore of identity – albeit with civic identity confined to small and sometimes exclusive geographic or social entities.

Given my own writing on Englishness and my work with Michael Wills and Gordon Brown on Britishness, it is not surprising that I embrace the thrust of this thesis: we should not be afraid of building a real alternative to narrow and defensive jingoism (or even what is now being called 'economic patriotism'). It is important that by building confidence we hold in common an affinity about what is good in our society – the 'glue' that holds together what would otherwise be disparate and dangerously individualistic libertarianism. It also allows us to head off the inevitable reaction to this libertarianism – fodder for the far right.

I think we may be getting into semantics over the issue of whether we can embrace 'values' as opposed to 'ideals' in this context. We strive for ideals; we understand values, even if they are so amorphous that it is difficult to narrow them down to more tangible and therefore graspable concepts. What some people see as the end of ideology is, in fact, a simple recognition of the complexity of the world we live in (with 24/7 news and information, satellite technology, the host of opportunities of access offered by web-based tools and ever greater mobility and economic liberalisation), which brings with it its own fears.

But what is remarkable, and is briefly alluded to in the essay, is the fact that we have actually made substantial progress in emerging from a bygone era. With the exception of the temporary swing to the right noted above, in the post 11 September period, it is remarkable how well people have coped with subliminal insecurity, the rapidity of economic and social change and the need to adjust to new forms of communication and mobility.

It is not clear, and this is an area for greater exploration, that European institutions have come to terms with the new global situation or have adjusted in any way to be able to assist people in their own community to handle such rapid change.

Here, the English language is key. David Goodhart rightly draws attention to my own challenge to Britain in the autumn of 2002, that a grasp of English by those seeking to integrate or even, more modestly, have a presence here, is essential – providing for us an environment where no one need walk out of European Council or conference venues, when one of our own British businessmen speaks in another's language!

Reciprocity is a critical issue raised in this essay. The early pioneers in the labour and trades union movement understood that 'something for something' (a favourite theme of mine) is essential, not only in getting people to be prepared to help each other, but also to reinforce solidarity and a sense of fairness. That is why the development of the welfare state and the move away from the friendly society or the local solution – while understandable and necessary in its time – also detached the contributor and the recipient from a common appreciation of the terms on which the 'contract' was to be agreed. In other words, if I am prepared to give up some of my money, I want to know that the person receiving it is not simply 'deserving' but is actually doing something themselves to use that support or opportunity to gain independence, or at the very least an appreciation of what contribution, if any, they can make in return.

Given the enormous commitment to volunteering and an enduring sense of community within Britain, there is real hope that we can develop civil (and civic) society in a way that underpins the transfer of cash, constituting the formal welfare state and, through the tax credits system, anti-poverty measures.

This is where (and I was glad that David Goodhart gave it a brief mention) identity cards play a part: not just in protecting a sense of identity, but actually ensuring that free public services are not abused, that the generous open policy for the right to work in this country – particularly for the new European states in central and eastern Europe – are not abused.

I am sure David Goodhart would want to play his part in building on the emerging but still frail foundation of greater honesty of the liberal left about how important security and stability is to the task of building openness and reducing fear of difference, thus ensuring that in the modern era issues around identity, sense of belonging and neighbourliness can be seen as a plus not as an oppressive sameness, fearing difference and suspicious of change.

But in doing this, I hope we will also recognise the essential nature of community and neighbourliness, of neighbourhood and of a bottom-up approach. We certainly will need leadership in identifying the strands which, if woven together, can not only hold society from disintegration, but actually provide the clothing of the body politic.

For ideas (or ideals) as a matter of fact are not enough. People have to know that the institutions, the processes, the day-to-day experiences of government at every level, are sensitive to their needs, but are also reflective of their fears. Creating mechanisms for delivery, changing historic patterns of thinking and behaviour, all of this is much more difficult than is ever normally acknowledged publicly. So in this debate, which I hope will continue vigorously, we need not only to reflect the fact that we have emerged from the immediate postimperial experience, but that in forging the future, we identify with, and have answers to offer, those who seek an identity and who wish for reassurance from our proud and tolerant, outward-facing and compassionate nation.

Let us hope that the World Cup offers an opportunity for pride without reaction, and that the build-up (as David Goodhart suggests) to the Olympic Games is an opportunity to reinforce a progressive and positive nationalism, which is inclusive and, as the presentation in winning the Olympic Games demonstrated so vigorously, a celebration of our vibrant and diverse nation!

David Blunkett is MP for Sheffield Brightside. He was education secretary from 1997 to 2001, home secretary from 2001 to 2004 and secretary for work and pensions in 2005. He is the author of Politics and Progress: Renewing democracy and civil society *(Methuen, 2001).*

John Denham

The debate on 'Britishness' and its relationship to progressive politics is only just beginning. A year ago those of us who thought the issue important tended to be met with scepticism and polite disinterest. Since then the debate has taken hold with real vigour. 2006 opened with a major speech by Gordon Brown on Britishness. It looks as though 'British identity' will be as central to the agenda of the next prime minister as it has been absent from the interests of the current one.

David Goodhart's essay is a challenging contribution to this developing debate. It is a marked change in tone from his earlier and controversial writings about diversity. These were suffused with deep pessimism about the prospects for Britain's multiracial society, founded on the erroneous idea that a diverse society was necessarily less cohesive. In truth, as he now makes clear, diversity may provide challenges but these are not intractable and may even provide opportunities to the left.

For most progressives, the identity debate is new. The collective process of sorting out the relevant from the irrelevant issues has only just begun. It is common to find sound arguments mixed with more contentious claims and this is true here.

Goodhart's description of why the left has ignored nationalism knocks down several straw men. (For example, I have never actually met anyone who believed that unlimited immigration was the correct recompense for colonial guilt.) And why is arranged marriage given so much attention in so many articles about British identity? Forced marriage is a crime and rightly so. Arranged marriage belongs to a different discussion about the implications of the whole diversity of relationships, cohabitation, high divorce rates and civil partnerships across our society. The implication that there is a 'British' way of doing these things is undermined by any quick look at the reality.

But such easy criticisms should not lead people to reject Goodhart's central thesis. National identity is important, the left needs to make it part of its project, and we need to start the debate on how to do it. The debate will be difficult, mistakes will be made and offence will be taken. But it must continue.

For most of my political life, the left has assumed that any strong British identity would be inimical to progressive politics. We certainly didn't think that our national identity was important to creating a fairer, more just society. And there are still plenty of people who hold that view. Much of the left is more comfortable dealing with the traditional agenda of equality, tackling social exclusion and opposing discrimination. In a very clear example of this a speaker from the Barrow Cadbury Trust told the Fabian conference[42] in January 2006: 'Sort out disadvantage and identity will look after itself.' This is simply not true.

These comfortable assumptions are now tumbling. It is clear that questions of identity, separate communities and disadvantage interact in potentially dangerous ways. Tackling disadvantage cannot guarantee success in dealing with the other issues; indeed, without taking on the challenges of identity and separate lives it is unlikely that disadvantage can be tackled successfully either.

Identity politics has not filled the gap left by class politics in quite the way David Goodhart suggests. As he mentions, but does not fully explore, some of the sharpest conflicts take place in and around the poorest communities and the labour markets in which they work. Here the impact of new, lower-cost migration hits the established poor (while making middle Britain better off). Here the competition for public resources and the social wage is sharpest. But identity politics stands in the way of disadvantaged communities seeing common interests. A society with a weak sense of any cohesive identity will necessarily find it more difficult to organise and sustain the collective responses that are needed not just to tackle disadvantage, but the welfare state, crime and security issues that dominate today's political agenda. Instead the door is opened to extremist political and faith organisations and, equally significant, inward-looking and sectional response to common concerns.

In other words, many of the issues that have traditionally been on the agenda for the left and centre cannot be tackled unless we can make progress on our collective national identity.

The process cannot be defined by minorities joining the majority; Britain has changed too much for that. The new British identity needs to tell a story about ourselves that works both for the majority and the minorities. That story will be created every bit as much as it can be discovered from the histories of the various people who inhabit these islands.

That seems to me to be the real challenge, but it is the most difficult part of the exercise and the one that needs most work. David Goodhart's central proposals for a progressive nationalism seem to rest on two ideas: we should have clearer definitions of who belongs, who does not and what each are entitled to; and we should develop better symbols of Britishness.

I agree with both propositions, but they will be limited in their impact.

It is good to debate the symbols of Britishness – flags, a national day and so on. We must ensure that the institutions that should symbolise Britain (parliament, the armed forces and the police among others) actually do represent all the different communities who live here. But without a modern national story it is difficult to understand what the symbols symbolise.

We should be far more sensitive to the impact of new migration on the poorest communities and their indigenous workforce. Sound migration controls need to be matched to better labour market regulation. The welfare state does need to be run on clear principles of rights and responsibilities, protected by proper systems to verify entitlement.

But important as these are, they are no substitute for developing the story of who we now are and who we now want to become. And this will be a diverse, collective effort involving ordinary people, musicians, historians, writers and broadcasters every bit as much as politicians. None of us can take part in this debate without revealing some of our own mistaken assumptions, misjudgements and misunderstandings of each other. That's why so many people don't want to have the debate at all. David Goodhart has been prepared to keep the debate going. We should all join in.

John Denham is Labour MP for Southampton Itchen and chair of the Home Affairs Select Committee.

Philippe Legrain

I know that socialism is a dirty word on the centre-left these days – but if David Goodhart had his way, nationalism would certainly no longer be.

It is one thing for someone on the centre-left to recognise reality – that national feelings still matter to most people to some degree – but it is quite another to argue that the government needs actively to rekindle a sense of nationalism, 'progressive' or otherwise. Leaving aside whether this is possible, what would be the aim? Goodhart argues that it is the 'best hope for preserving the social democratic virtues embodied in a generous welfare state and a thriving public domain'. In essence, he fears that immigration, greater mobility and increased individualism threaten to undermine support for a universal welfare state, which therefore needs to be shored up by fostering a sense of nationalism that strengthens our feelings of solidarity towards our fellow citizens. Underlying his concerns is a belief that community feeling is inexorably weakening. In both respects, I think he is mistaken.

I can scarcely do justice to such big topics in only a thousand words, but as I argue in my forthcoming book on immigration, the welfare state is not threatened in the way Goodhart thinks it is, nor does continued support for it require, or even necessarily follow from, a strengthening of nationalism. Just look at the generosity of welfare provision in super-diverse Canada or hyper-diverse Toronto – or compare cosmopolitan, social-democratic London with the patriotic Tory shires.

Goodhart is, of course, right that people are often willing to be more generous towards those for whom they feel a sense of solidarity – and that one basis for this might be a common national identity – but the welfare state is based on more than just solidarity, and solidarity can be based on many things other than nationalism. Conversely, nationalistic societies need not be full of brotherly love, while cosmopolitan societies may be more compassionate.

One can feel a strong sense of solidarity for people who live in the same place rather than belong to the same nation. No doubt the shared experience of the 7 July bombings and the ongoing common threat of terrorism have increased Londoners' concern for each other. Political beliefs are important, too: socialists support stronger government action to help others than conservatives do; but, although Americans are generally more patriotic than Britons, this does not translate into support for government welfare programmes.

Moreover, the welfare state need not be based on national citizenship: in the US and Canada it is primarily organised at a state or provincial level, with welfare provision varying widely according to local preferences and with eligibility typically a function of residence or contributions, since state or provincial citizenship does not exist. Thus if the British state were less centralised, one could easily envisage an autonomous London region having a generous welfare state, paid for by those working in London for those living in London and independent of their national citizenship(s).

In any case, solidarity is by no means the sole basis for social provision. The universal welfare state also provides the rich with security against the poor – and provides everyone with security against unemployment, illness and old age. After all, European welfare states stem not only from socialism and compassion, but also from fear: enlightened elites tried to buy off the masses to stave off revolution. Indeed, you may loathe your jobless neighbour but still be willing to pay for unemployment benefits if you fear that he might otherwise rob you – or that you might one day end up out of work yourself. People support the NHS not just out of concern that all should have access to healthcare, but mainly out of self-interest – because they believe a government-funded healthcare system works out cheaper and better for them than a private insurance system would. A society with less solidarity could still support the NHS.

Underlying Goodhart's nationalist prospectus is the belief that community feeling is weakening. Yet he appears to have a very narrow vision of society that romanticises a particular type of community: national society and old-fashioned working-class communities. He asserts, for instance, that: 'It is the core belief of the left, against the individualism of free-market liberals, that there is such a thing as society – but in the modern world that always, everywhere, means a specific national society.' This is nonsense on stilts. Everyone is torn between the urge to do their own thing and the need to live with others: individual choice therefore exists largely within a framework of the aggregated individual choices made by others – 'society'. In this context, 'society' can mean everything from a family to a group of friends, a workplace, a village, an urban neighbourhood, a national society that sets its own laws, or a global sense of humanity that aspires to common norms such as human rights.

So it is simply not true that: 'the alternative to a mild, progressive nationalism is not internationalism, which will always be a minority creed, but either chauvinistic nationalism or the absence of any broader solidarities at all.' Misplaced nostalgia for the erosion of the coerced local communities of old – the flipside of which is liberation from the tyranny of geography, social immobility and the straitjacket of imposed national uniformity – should not blind us to the richness and vibrancy of the new chosen communities, be they groups of friends from different backgrounds, multinational workplaces, environmental campaigns that span the globe, or online networks of people with a common interest. Solidarity is alive and well when British volunteer doctors treat AIDS sufferers in Africa, when friends take over many of the roles that family members once performed (or failed to perform), and when the membership of pressure groups never ceases to rise. We don't need a new-fangled nationalism for society to thrive.

Philippe Legrain is a journalist and writer. His book on global migration will be published in late 2006 or early 2007 (see www.philippelegrain.com).

Bhikhu Parekh

I agree with much of Goodhart's thoughtful and wide-ranging essay. He is right to emphasise the importance of a strong sense of community, a quasi-contractual view of citizenship, fairness as the basis of social trust, a generous welfare state, and a capacious view of national identity. His essay also contains several sensible practical suggestions, some of which are novel and imaginative and worth implementing.

My disagreement with him is threefold. First, his essay becomes narrower and one-sided as it proceeds. He claims to address security and identity issues, but has little to say about the former, especially violent crime, rising incivility and social fragmentation. Tackling them requires strong and self-disciplining local communities, which could form the building blocks of the national community and make Britain a community of communities. Goodhart does not explore how this vital objective is to be achieved.

So far as the identity issues are concerned, Goodhart's otherwise perceptive discussion suffers from the fact that he sees them largely through the narrow prism of immigration. On several occasions when he deals with important questions such as the need for fairness and national solidarity, he slips into a discussion of immigration. He thereby conveys the unwitting impression that immigration is a major threat to our national identity and solidarity, precisely the point made by the BNP and right-wing nationalists. Goodhart clearly does not share the view, but his way of formulating the problem renders him vulnerable to such an unkind interpretation. Furthermore, this way of seeing the problem blinds him to the deeper crisis of British society. Its lack of moral consensus, social breakdown, resentful and marginalised groups who lack a stake in society and find solace in mindless chauvinism at home and especially abroad would remain even if all the immigrants were to leave the country. These questions cry out for a patient and probing analysis, to which Goodhart's undue preoccupation with immigration prevents him from giving adequate attention.

Second, Goodhart's discussion of the issues relating to citizenship and national solidarity contains serious gaps. Although the welfare state expresses and reinforces and is vital for national solidarity, the latter is largely passive. People might dutifully discharge their part of the contract, work hard, play fair and so on, but that does not by itself draw them out of themselves and create a vibrant and proud community. How do we achieve this? Goodhart talks of British 'ideals', but does not say what these are, how they differ from Gordon Brown's 'values', and whether there is or can be a national consensus on them. He talks of a coherent national story, preferably a Whiggish view of national history. But this is only one story among several. Tories won't share it; nor would immigrants and the radical left because of its failure to offer a balanced account of the British Empire. He wants our identity to be defined in cultural rather than political terms as is the case today, but does not say what that involves and whether it is not likely to be too exclusive to accommodate legitimate diversity.

National solidarity is created and sustained when citizens actively appropriate their local and national communities through political participation, come together to debate local and national issues, and develop a shared sense of ownership of their community. In the absence of such a vivid and constantly affirmed sense of collective ownership, citizens remain atomised, and all attempts to unite them into a genuine political community through formal means remain precarious. While Goodhart is right to stress welfare rights and social 'hardware' and 'software', he ignores the equally important question of narrowing the growing distance between the state and the citizens by suitably restructuring our political institutions.

This leads me to my third difficulty. Goodhart seeks a much stronger degree of unity and solidarity than a liberal state can offer, and freely uses the language of nationalism. Despite his valiant efforts to escape its collectivist logic, he remains trapped in it. He talks of 'integrationism' which, apart from being an inelegant mouthful, has an ominous logic. He does not want Asians to find their spouses in the subcontinent, though presumably their white counterparts face no such restriction. If one complains that this interferes with their most personal choices, violates their fundamental rights, and discriminates against them, Goodhart rejoins that integration is an 'inherently illiberal process'. One shudders to think what else 'integrationism' involves, especially in less liberal hands. He uses the fashionable language of 'glue' as if human beings could be stuck together through some adhesive into a 'cohesive' whole. He talks of 'Britishness' as if being British is not a relational category signifying mutual commitment but a quality, like redness or sweetness, that all British people must uniformly share. His discussion of immigrants is almost entirely in economic terms, and ignores their great contributions to our cuisine, arts, literature, sports and intellectual life, a common feature of much nationalist thought.

Goodhart wants all citizens, long established and especially new, to 'accept the national norms' on such things as the role of religion in society and free speech. They should certainly not resort to violence, but can't they at least question these norms and provoke a public debate? What justifies such an arbitrary closure? Are we so convinced that we have got the balance absolutely right? Goodhart wants Britain to select highly skilled immigrants from poor countries. And as for the excluded unskilled ones, he wants Britain to help their countries through aid and fair trade rules. This is a strange way to show international solidarity. Aid and fair trade rules, as we well know, always remain precarious and are no more than a pious wish in the current climate; and such aid as we might give often falls far short of the reverse aid the poor countries give us in the form of fully trained labour. It is ironic that this is justified in the name of 'progressive' nationalism and centre-left morality.

The language of nationalism is deeply flawed and best avoided. This is as true of its civic and liberal variety as of its discredited ethnic cousin. The culturally based civic nationalism of France cannot accommodate the *hijab* and much else, and its constitutionally based American counterpart once felt threatened by 'un-American' activities and is now frightened of 'unpatriotic' dissent. Happily Britain has no such problem partly because, as Goodhart says, it is 'not a nation at all but a state' or rather an open and relaxed political community. Goodhart is anxious to turn it into one, and that is the wrong way to go.

Professor Lord Bhikhu Parekh is a professor at the Centre for the Study of Democracy at the University of Westminster and emeritus professor of political theory at the University of Hull. He was chair of the Commission on the Future of Multi-Ethnic Britain, whose report was published in October 2000. Professor Parekh was appointed to the House of Lords in March 2000.

Notes

1   W Bos, 'After Van Gogh', *Prospect*, Jan 2005.
2   I prefer in this paper to use the word nationalism, rather than patriotism, but
    then to distinguish it from chauvinistic nationalism by qualifying it with the
    adjectives progressive or enlightened. It is a reminder that there is a nationalism
    spectrum but also that nations are things that still have boundaries even if they
    are more porous than they used to be.
3   G Monbiot, 'The new chauvinism', *Guardian*, 9 Aug 2005.
4   D Goodhart, 'Too diverse?', *Prospect*, Feb 2004.
5   RSA Migration Commission Report, *Migration: A welcome opportunity – a new
    way forward by the RSA Migration Commission* (London: Royal Society for the
    Encouragement of Arts, Manufactures & Commerce, 2005), available at
    www.migrationcommission.org/publications.htm (accessed 1 May 2006).
6   A Heath, 'Is a sense of British identity in decline?', *Devolution Briefings* no 36
    (ESRC, Aug 2005), available at www.devolution.ac.uk/Briefing_papers.htm
    (accessed 1 May 2006).
7   The interaction between or even conflict between a revival of Britishness and
    Englishness is a large subject in its own right that I do not try to tackle here.
8   The Office for National Statistics (ONS) reports that 11% of the British
    population moved home in 2000.
9   One study compared crime and health outcomes where people know their
    neighbours and where they don't. See I Kawachi, B Kennedy and R Wilkinson,
    'Crime: social disorganization and relative deprivation', *Social Science and
    Medicine* vol 48 (1999).
10 'Crime in England and Wales 2004/2005', *British Crime Survey* (London: Home
    Office, 2005).
11 B Parekh, 'British commitments', *Prospect*, Sep 2005.
12 MORI poll Commission for Racial Equality, 'Race is no barrier to "being
    British", but there is no consistent sense of "Britishness"', (London: MORI, May
    2002), see www.mori.com/polls/2002/cre.shtml (accessed 1 May 2006).

13   S Exley et al, *British Social Attitudes 2000 Survey Technical Report* (London: National Centre for Social Research, 2003).

14   R Colls, *Identity of England* (Oxford: Oxford University Press, 2002).

15   T Modood, 'Remaking multiculturalism after 7/7', *Open Democracy*, 29 Sep 2005.

16   D Miller, 'Immigration, nations and citizenship', paper presented at a conference 5–6 July 2004, sponsored by the Centre for Research in the Arts, Social Sciences and Humanities (CRASSH), University of Cambridge, Cambridge, UK.

17   According to a BBC/ICM poll of December 2002, 26% of Muslims felt not very or not at all loyal towards Britain. And various polls have found between 7% and 15% of British Muslims saying that the 9/11 attacks were justified. See www.icmresearch.co.uk/reviews/2002/bbc-today-muslims-dec-02.htm (accessed 4 May 2006).

18   T Cantle, *The End of Parallel Lives? The report of the Community Cohesion Panel* (London: Home Office, 2004).

19   T Modood, *Multicultural Politics: Racism, ethnicity and Muslims in Britain* (Edinburgh: Edinburgh University Press, 2005).

20   P Taylor-Gooby, 'Is the future American? Or can left politics preserve European welfare states from erosion through growing "racial" diversity?', *Journal of Social Policy*, Dec 2005.

21   J Salt and J Clarke, 'Migration matters', *Prospect*, May 2005.

22   Mervyn King, speech delivered at Salts Mill, Bradford, 13 June 2005.

23   J Cruddas et al, *The Far Right in London: A challenge to local democracy?* (York: Joseph Rowntree Reform Trust, 2005).

24   *Prospect* and MORI poll, *Prospect*, Feb 2004.

25   G Dench, K Gavron and M Young, *The New East End: Kinship, race and conflict* (London: Profile, 2006).

26   Ibid.

27   Ibid.

28   J Denham, 'The fairness code', *Prospect*, June 2004.

29   According to the Home Office there are thought to be between 310,000 and 570,000 illegal immigrants currently living in Britain.

30   The ONS has revised upwards the estimated population for 2031 from today's 60–67 million, with most of the increase due directly or indirectly to immigration.

31   RSA Migration Commission Report, *Migration*.

32   Denham, 'Fairness code'.

33   Ibid.

34   The most popular US entitlement programme is the GI Bill, which grants student loans, housing benefits and other rewards to veterans of the military and their children.

35   S Rushdie, 'What this cultural debate needs is more dirt, less pure stupidity', *The Times*, 10 Dec 2005, available at www.timesonline.co.uk/article/0,,1072-1918306,00.html (accessed 2 May 2006).

36   E Kaufmann, *The Rise and Fall of Anglo-America* (Cambridge, MA: Harvard University Press, 2004).

37 Cantle, *The End of Parallel Lives?*

38 Goodhart, 'Too diverse?'

39 Tom Nairn, 'A myriad byzantiums', *New Left Review* no 23 (second series), Sept/Oct 2003.

40 With considerable support from Nick Pearce, now director of ippr, see *Politics and Progress? Renewing democracy and civil society* (London, Methuen, 2001).

41 Secretary of State for the Home Department, *Secure Borders, Safe Haven: Integration with diversity in modern Britain*, nationality and immigration white paper (Cm 5387) (Norwich: The Stationery Office, February 2002).

42 Fabian New Year Conference 2006, 'Who do we want to be? The future of Britishness', Imperial College, London, 14 Jan 2006.

DEMOS – Licence to Publish

1. **Definitions**
   a **"Collective Work"** means a work, such as a periodical issue, anthology or encyclopedia, in which the Work in its entirety in unmodified form, along with a number of other contributions, constituting separate and independent works in themselves, are assembled into a collective whole. A work that constitutes a Collective Work will not be considered a Derivative Work (as defined below) for the purposes of this Licence.
   b **"Derivative Work"** means a work based upon the Work or upon the Work and other pre-existing works, such as a musical arrangement, dramatization, fictionalization, motion picture version, sound recording, art reproduction, abridgment, condensation, or any other form in which the Work may be recast, transformed, or adapted, except that a work that constitutes a Collective Work or a translation from English into another language will not be considered a Derivative Work for the purpose of this Licence.
   c **"Licensor"** means the individual or entity that offers the Work under the terms of this Licence.
   d **"Original Author"** means the individual or entity who created the Work.
   e **"Work"** means the copyrightable work of authorship offered under the terms of this Licence.
   f **"You"** means an individual or entity exercising rights under this Licence who has not previously violated the terms of this Licence with respect to the Work, or who has received express permission from DEMOS to exercise rights under this Licence despite a previous violation.
2. **Fair Use Rights.** Nothing in this licence is intended to reduce, limit, or restrict any rights arising from fair use, first sale or other limitations on the exclusive rights of the copyright owner under copyright law or other applicable laws.
3. **Licence Grant.** Subject to the terms and conditions of this Licence, Licensor hereby grants You a worldwide, royalty-free, non-exclusive, perpetual (for the duration of the applicable copyright) licence to exercise the rights in the Work as stated below:
   a to reproduce the Work, to incorporate the Work into one or more Collective Works, and to reproduce the Work as incorporated in the Collective Works;
   b to distribute copies or phonorecords of, display publicly, perform publicly, and perform publicly by means of a digital audio transmission the Work including as incorporated in Collective Works;
   The above rights may be exercised in all media and formats whether now known or hereafter devised. The above rights include the right to make such modifications as are technically necessary to exercise the rights in other media and formats. All rights not expressly granted by Licensor are hereby reserved.
4. **Restrictions.** The licence granted in Section 3 above is expressly made subject to and limited by the following restrictions:
   a You may distribute, publicly display, publicly perform, or publicly digitally perform the Work only under the terms of this Licence, and You must include a copy of, or the Uniform Resource Identifier for, this Licence with every copy or phonorecord of the Work You distribute, publicly display, publicly perform, or publicly digitally perform. You may not offer or impose any terms on the Work that alter or restrict the terms of this Licence or the recipients' exercise of the rights granted hereunder. You may not sublicence the Work. You must keep intact all notices that refer to this Licence and to the disclaimer of warranties. You may not distribute, publicly display, publicly perform, or publicly digitally perform the Work with any technological measures that control access or use of the Work in a manner inconsistent with the terms of this Licence Agreement. The above applies to the Work as incorporated in a Collective Work, but this does not require the Collective Work apart from the Work itself to be made subject to the terms of this Licence. If You create a Collective Work, upon notice from any Licencor You must, to the extent practicable, remove from the Collective Work any reference to such Licensor or the Original Author, as requested.
   b You may not exercise any of the rights granted to You in Section 3 above in any manner that is primarily intended for or directed toward commercial advantage or private monetary

compensation. The exchange of the Work for other copyrighted works by means of digital file-sharing or otherwise shall not be considered to be intended for or directed toward commercial advantage or private monetary compensation, provided there is no payment of any monetary compensation in connection with the exchange of copyrighted works.

c   If you distribute, publicly display, publicly perform, or publicly digitally perform the Work or any Collective Works, You must keep intact all copyright notices for the Work and give the Original Author credit reasonable to the medium or means You are utilizing by conveying the name (or pseudonym if applicable) of the Original Author if supplied; the title of the Work if supplied. Such credit may be implemented in any reasonable manner; provided, however, that in the case of a Collective Work, at a minimum such credit will appear where any other comparable authorship credit appears and in a manner at least as prominent as such other comparable authorship credit.

5. Representations, Warranties and Disclaimer

a   By offering the Work for public release under this Licence, Licensor represents and warrants that, to the best of Licensor's knowledge after reasonable inquiry:

  i   Licensor has secured all rights in the Work necessary to grant the licence rights hereunder and to permit the lawful exercise of the rights granted hereunder without You having any obligation to pay any royalties, compulsory licence fees, residuals or any other payments;

  ii The Work does not infringe the copyright, trademark, publicity rights, common law rights or any other right of any third party or constitute defamation, invasion of privacy or other tortious injury to any third party.

b   EXCEPT AS EXPRESSLY STATED IN THIS LICENCE OR OTHERWISE AGREED IN WRITING OR REQUIRED BY APPLICABLE LAW, THE WORK IS LICENCED ON AN "AS IS" BASIS, WITHOUT WARRANTIES OF ANY KIND, EITHER EXPRESS OR IMPLIED INCLUDING, WITHOUT LIMITATION, ANY WARRANTIES REGARDING THE CONTENTS OR ACCURACY OF THE WORK.

6. Limitation on Liability. EXCEPT TO THE EXTENT REQUIRED BY APPLICABLE LAW, AND EXCEPT FOR DAMAGES ARISING FROM LIABILITY TO A THIRD PARTY RESULTING FROM BREACH OF THE WARRANTIES IN SECTION 5, IN NO EVENT WILL LICENSOR BE LIABLE TO YOU ON ANY LEGAL THEORY FOR ANY SPECIAL, INCIDENTAL, CONSEQUENTIAL, PUNITIVE OR EXEMPLARY DAMAGES ARISING OUT OF THIS LICENCE OR THE USE OF THE WORK, EVEN IF LICENSOR HAS BEEN ADVISED OF THE POSSIBILITY OF SUCH DAMAGES.

7. Termination

a   This Licence and the rights granted hereunder will terminate automatically upon any breach by You of the terms of this Licence. Individuals or entities who have received Collective Works from You under this Licence, however, will not have their licences terminated provided such individuals or entities remain in full compliance with those licences. Sections 1, 2, 5, 6, 7, and 8 will survive any termination of this Licence.

b   Subject to the above terms and conditions, the licence granted here is perpetual (for the duration of the applicable copyright in the Work). Notwithstanding the above, Licensor reserves the right to release the Work under different licence terms or to stop distributing the Work at any time; provided, however that any such election will not serve to withdraw this Licence (or any other licence that has been, or is required to be, granted under the terms of this Licence), and this Licence will continue in full force and effect unless terminated as stated above.

8. Miscellaneous

a   Each time You distribute or publicly digitally perform the Work or a Collective Work, DEMOS offers to the recipient a licence to the Work on the same terms and conditions as the licence granted to You under this Licence.

b   If any provision of this Licence is invalid or unenforceable under applicable law, it shall not affect the validity or enforceability of the remainder of the terms of this Licence, and without further action by the parties to this agreement, such provision shall be reformed to the minimum extent necessary to make such provision valid and enforceable.

c   No term or provision of this Licence shall be deemed waived and no breach consented to unless such waiver or consent shall be in writing and signed by the party to be charged with such waiver or consent.

d   This Licence constitutes the entire agreement between the parties with respect to the Work licensed here. There are no understandings, agreements or representations with respect to the Work not specified here. Licensor shall not be bound by any additional provisions that may appear in any communication from You. This Licence may not be modified without the mutual written agreement of DEMOS and You.